THE LUTHERAN DOCTRINE OF THE LORD'S SUPPER

THE SCRIPTURAL CHARACTER OF THE LUTHERAN DOCTRINE OF THE LORD'S SUPPER.

BY THE REV. H. I. SCHMIDT, D.D.

THE SCRIPTURAL CHARACTER OF THE LUTHERAN DOCTRINE OF THE LORD'S SUPPER

Just & Sinner
1467 Walnut Ave.
Brighton, IA 52540

www.JustandSinner.com

ISBN 10: 0615899943
ISBN 13: 978-0615899947

TABLE OF CONTENTS

INTRODUCTION 9

CHAPTER 1: HISTORICAL INTRODUCTION 13
11

CHAPTER 2: THE SCRIPTURAL CHARACTER OF 31
THE LUTHERAN DOCTRINE

CHAPTER 3: FIGURATIVE LANGUAGE AND THE 37
WORDS OF INSTITUTION

CHAPTER 4: THE REAL PRESENCE AND HUMAN 47
REASON

CHAPTER 5: THE WORDS OF INSTITUTION AND 55
CHRIST'S GLORIFIED BODY

CHAPTER 6: THE OMNIPRESENCE OF CHRIST 65

CHAPTER 7: THE CHARGE OF "CARNAL EATING" 77

CHAPTER 8: THE EUCHARIST IN 1 CORINTHIANS 79

CHAPTER 9: THE COMMUNICATION OF 85
ATTRIBUTES

CHAPTER 10: THE EUCHARIST IN JOHN 6 97

CHAPTER 11: LUTHERAN CHRISTOLOGY 105

CHAPTER 12: CONCLUDING ARGUMENTS 117

INTRODUCTION

THE nineteenth century was definitive in the establishment of Lutheran identity in North America. With a nation that was influenced by Puritanism, and later Revivalism, many Lutherans wondered if it was possible to retain their Lutheran identity in the midst of the culture of the new world. Some supported union between Lutheran and Reformed churches, being willing to give up a distinctively Lutheran identity, whereas others fought to protect Lutheran theology and practice.

There is no area where this struggle is more evident than in the doctrine of the Lord's Supper. The affirmation of the real presence of Christ in the Eucharist has been a distinguishing mark of the Lutheran church over against the Reformed and Arminian traditions. Since Luther refused to take Zwingli's hand at the Marburg colloquy, this teaching has divided the Lutheran and Reformed traditions.

The theology of Samuel S. Schmucker was at the heart of the debates about Lutheran identity in nineteenth century America. Schmucker was a German immigrant, who, having been raised in it, claimed the Lutheran theological tradition as his own. He studied at the notably Reformed Princeton Seminary, and was ordained as a Lutheran minister in 1820. Schmucker later became an influential professor at

Gettysburg College and helped found the "General Synod." Although continuing to claim the Lutheran perspective, Schmucker argued that some Lutheran teachings, as found in the Confessions, were in error. Chief among these was the historically Lutheran doctrine of Holy Communion: that Christ is present in, with, and under the Eucharistic elements. This caused him to publish a revised version of the Augsburg Confession which left out those portions that would be offensive to the Reformed community. This modified confession was rejected by his own synod. The present work is a response to the claims made by Schmucker against the traditional Lutheran doctrine of Holy Communion.

The author, Henry Immanuel Schmidt, was born in Nazareth Pennsylvania in 1806. He became an ordained minister in the New York Ministerium in 1829, and served churches in Pennsylvania and Boston. Schmidt was a noted theologian and professor, teaching at Hartwick Seminary, Pennsylvania College, Gettysburg, and finally at Columbia College in New York. He was a frequent contributor to the Lutheran periodical *The Evangelical Review*, which is where his writing on the present subject began. He was also a friend and father figure to the notable Lutheran theologian, Charles Krauth.

Schmidt's writing in this volume is a defense of the historic Lutheran position on Holy Communion. He begins his thesis by demonstrating that the doctrine of the real presence of Christ is the historic Christian position by citing various church fathers on the issue. He then takes Schmidt to task, answering his objections point by point. Schmucker's arguments were not new. They are the same arguments that the Reformed tradition has used against the Lutheran church since the sixteenth century. Because they are the same arguments often made today, this work is a helpful study in the defense of traditional Lutheran teaching. Schmidt discusses the words of institution, the nature of figurative language, the omnipresence of Christ, the words of Paul in 1

Corinthians, and the communication of attributes from the divine to the human nature in Christ.

This volume has endured a significant amount of editing. The original work was lacking citations of any of the Patristic quotes, was full of untranslated Greek, Latin, and German phrases, contained no chapter breaks, and often extended a single paragraph for several pages. I have attempted to make this work readable while retaining as much of the author's own style and language as possible. I have translated much of the Greek, some of the Latin terms, and cut out unnecessary German phrases which frequently appeared next to their English translation. Hopefully this allows the volume to be more useful and edifying as a defense of the presence of our Lord in his Holy Supper.

Jordan Cooper
2013

CHAPTER 1
HISTORICAL INTRODUCTION

THE essay which is published here as a separate book first appeared in the quarterly Evangelical Review (Issue 10, Article 2, October, 1851). This separate republication has been extensively called for due to the confines of the article's previous design. A more extended brief history thus should be premised.

There are many reasons for regarding a historic view of our doctrine as invaluable at the present time. It is important to show that in the views respecting the Lord's Supper, which Luther so clearly and fully stated, and so ably defended, he propounded nothing new, but simply reasserted and vindicated, in opposition to the errors and perversions of Romanism, the doctrinal views of the early church, and above all, the sense of Holy Scripture, conveyed in most direct and simple language.

It is important to show that in our interpretation of the words of the institution, and of the language of St. Paul, we have on our side not only the expositions given by the early Church Fathers in general, but the simple and strictly scriptural interpretations of those in particular, who immediately succeeded the apostolic age, and derived their views from the apostles themselves. It is even more important to point out this connection, because, even if these primitive Fathers deserved to be looked upon with particular suspicion, which we deny, there could be, in respect of the subject here discussed, no motive to change, to distort, or in any way to pervert and corrupt, the teachings which they had received directly from one or more of our Lord's apostles.

In matters pertaining to the polity and discipline, to the general government of the church, we may safely admit, without any serious disparagement to the clergy of the first two centuries, that human passions, motives of self-interest, and self-glorification may have led, even at that early age, gradually and perhaps imperceptibly, to arbitrary arrangements and assumptions of authority that were not borne out by the sanction of Scripture. But, so much were the circumstances and wants of the infant church calculated to throw power into the hands of her pastors and teachers, that it does not seem just to charge the gradually increasing importance and growing authority of the clergy to their own ambitions and schemes and measures.

However this may be, there is no evidence and no reason to believe, that in the primitive ages of the church the doctrines of Christianity suffered any corruption within her pale; on the other hand, we are certain that the early Fathers were the staunch and faithful protectors and defenders of the pure and uncorrupted truths of the gospel, in opposition to the speculative theologians and heretics who sought, in various ways, to modify and pervert them. Doctrinal corruptions within the church were of later growth, and it was not until the hierarchy of Rome was fully established that it occurred to ambitious priests and arrogant bishops, that the sacraments might be effectually employed as means of exalting their personal importance and increasing their official dignity and power; and to render them thus subservient, the doctrines of scripture regarding them were either distorted, or weighed down by human inventions.

However, on subjects of this kind we may safely regard the early church as holding and promulgating the genuine doctrines of Scripture, and the just and sound views which she had received directly from the lips of inspired apostles. Hence, we deem it important to trace the views respecting the Lord's Supper, which, taught by our symbolical books, are presented and defended in the following treatise, up to that early age, in which the doctrinal corruptions which, after ages of pampered prosperity and priestly arrogance super induced, were still unknown. And that this we are able to do, it is our present business to show somewhat more in detail than our limited space permitted in the following essay. We merely remark that, although we have a number of important authorities before us, we are mainly indebted for much that follows here to Guericke's *Handbuch der Kirchengeschichte.*

We assert then, that the church has, at all times, from the very beginning, held and declared the belief, that in the sacrament of the altar the real (not figurative) body and blood of the Savior are truly present, distributed to communicants, and received by true believers to their unspeakable comfort and edification, their establishment, confirmation and advancement in that spiritual life, of which Christ within them is the vital principle and the very essence. No opposite, no other[1] view ever received ecclesiastical sanction until the Reformed church, the church of which Calvin and Zwingli were the founders, was organized. On this point, the evidence of history is clear and conclusive. Let us then look back to the beginning, and thereafter carry out our view over the historic page down to the present time.

From the earliest times the church regarded and celebrated the Lord's Supper, not as a mere memorial feast, commemorative of the sufferings and death of her Lord, but

---

[1] For the Romish doctrine of transubstantiation, being a clumsy attempt rigidly and minutely to define the mode of Christ's presence in the Eucharist, is only a monstrous distortion, not a denial of the truth. It distorts, not by taking away, but by adding. The church of Rome goes far beyond the truth, while Zwinglians and others deny it, in open contradiction of Scripture and of the testimony of the early church.

as a most sacred mystery, as the highest mystery of the Christian worship, because it effected a mysterious union between Christ and his people through the presence and reception of his body and blood. Hence from it were excluded all unrepentant; and hence also arose the false accusations of the heathens: that in this supper Christians partook of Thyestian meals and ate human flesh. Athenagoras most ably defended against these absurd charges in his well-known apology. This accusation is one of those extraneous testimonies, of which the hostility of Pagans and Jews furnishes not a few; although a gross caricature of the truth, it proves by its very presence the existence and prevalence of the doctrine caricatured. (p. 14-15)

The same view which was obviously universal in the early church is distinctly implied in the language employed by Ignatius, when, in the 20th chapter of his epistle to the Ephesians, and in the 7th of his epistle to the church at Smyrna, he sets forth the nature of the Eucharist. This Father, whose praise was in all the early churches, was a disciple and a companion of the apostles; he was instructed in Christian truth probably by either Peter or John. In the epistles just referred to, he calls the Eucharist a medicine unto immorality, an antidote against death through which we live evermore in Christ. He warns against the Docetists, who abstained from the Lord's Supper because they refused to acknowledge that, "It is the flesh or our Redeemer Jesus Christ."[2] Of course these heretics could not oppose a doctrine that did not exist.

Still more full and direct is the testimony of Justin Martyr, born A.D. 89, and martyred A.D. 163, or 165. He was the first apologist of Christianity, and declares in his apology that the language quoted here expresses the faith and confession of the church. Respecting the Eucharist he says: "We receive it not as common bread or as common

---

[2] Ignatius, Epistle to the Smyrneans 6:2

drink...but we have been taught that it is the flesh and blood of the incarnate Jesus."[3]

To the same effect, Irenaeus, who studied in Smyrna under Polycarp, the disciple of St. John, and died A.D. 209, as bishop of Lyons, expresses himself in his celebrated work Against Heresies, written about A.D. 107, as follows:

> The terrestrial bread, when through the invocation of God it has been consecrated, it is no more common bread, but the Eucharist, which consists of two constituents, the one earthly, the other heavenly.[4]

From this he deduces the future raising up of the body, "inasmuch as through Christ's body the germ of incorruptibility is deposited within us."

The testimony of the Fathers respecting the doctrinal views inculcated, and the doctrinal expositions given by the apostles themselves, depends, for its value and weight of authority, in a good degree on their greater or less proximity to the age concerning which they bear witness. It is obvious that here the three Fathers whom we have just cited are the most important, not only because they are the oldest in whose writings the Lord's Supper is mentioned, but because the sphere of labor which they respectively occupied in the church afforded them particular advantages for ascertaining and communicating the faith of the primitive church, in respect of doctrines which were afterwards made subjects of controversy.

Ignatius, who is very properly regarded as a disciple of the school of the apostle John, resided in Asia Minor, which, as the theater of the labors of the apostles John and Paul, stood in the highest estimation, as having preserved in its purity the earliest form of Christianity.[5] We have already

---

[3] Justin Martyr, First Apology 66
[4] Irenaeus, Against Heresies Book IV, 18:4-5
[5] See: Irenaeus, Against Heresies III,3

remarked that he was a friend of Polycarp, who, according to the most authentic primitive tradition, was a pupil of the apostle John. Irenaeus, also from Asia Minor, had likewise known and heard Polycarp; and thus also Justin had, during his journeys, become acquainted with the prominent churches in Asia Minor. Their decided and remarkable agreement both in the doctrine and in the manner of expressing it is therefore of the utmost importance and, "must convince us that we have here the original doctrine concerning the Lord's Supper, derived directly from the apostles themselves."[6]

To the same effect might be cited the ancient liturgical formulas, for the celebration of the Lord's Supper, especially one, which is ascribed to the Apostle James; but it may suffice to refer the reader for information on this point, to Guericke's *Handbuch der Kirchengeschichte*, Vol. I. p. 199. We may also appeal to Tertullian and Cyprian, and others, as avowing, only more distinctly and fully, the same view of the Lord's Supper as that set forth in the writings of those primitive Fathers; but, having the testimony of the latter, we do not consider it necessary to quote the language of any who wrote at a later period.--What we want to show, is, that the primitive church held the view of the Lord's Supper which is taught by the symbolical books of the Lutheran church, and this we have satisfactorily done. Later changes in the doctrinal system of the church cannot at all affect our argument; but such changes did not come quickly.

For, from the beginning of the fourth to near the end of the sixth century, the real presence of the body and blood of Christ in the Eucharist, so clearly recognized in the period just partially reviewed, was even more decidedly and explicitly avowed and confessed, as can be amply demonstrated from the liturgies of this period. We are simply forbidden by the confines of this writing to quote from these liturgies, and to

---

[6] See H.L. Heubner's Supplement to the 6th Edition of G. Buchner's Biblical House-Concodrance: Halle, 1845, Article, Lord's Supper, p. 3, sq.

cite the overabundant testimonies of the Fathers of this period. We refer the reader again for ample information to Guericke's *Handbauch der Kirchengeschichte*, Vol. I. p. 404. But it was during this period also that, in the explicit and distinct manner in which the doctrine was expressed in the sacramental liturgies, the Lord's Supper began to be gradually regarded as a sacrificial act of the Christian priest, and, in connection with this view, others which we must regard as erroneous, developed themselves into shape and distinctness. Prominent among these was the notion of its being an *oblatio pro mortuis*—a sacrificial act repeating the death of the Redeemer—by which departed souls could be delivered from purgatory. This absurd view began to prevail more and more, and was particularly indebted to Gregory the Great, who not only decided that it belonged essentially to the doctrine of the Lord's Supper, but rendered it popular by imaginative and elaborate representations of its practical value.

Out of this notion grew, in the eighth century, the private or solitary masses, celebrated by the priest alone, notwithstanding that bishops and councils protested against the abuse so late even as the ninth century. The want of dogmatical distinctness and definiteness in stating the doctrine of the Church, which must always prevail, to a greater or less degree, until systematic divinity has become settled, could not fail to lead to discussions and to provoke controversies. It is unnecessary here to enter into specifications respecting these; the less so as in one most important point of view, they will be fully exhibited in a translation of Thomasius' *Christologie* which we intend shortly to publish. It will suffice to say, that the view which denies the real presence of Christ's body and blood in the Eucharist never acquired any firm footing or extensive influence in the church: its only distinguished defender was Berengarius de Tours,[7] a man whose repeated equivocations and recantations

---

[7] For information on Bernagarius, see: Radding, Charles M. and Francis Newton. *Theology, Rhetoric, and Politics in the Eucharistic Controversy, 1078-*

prove him so utterly destitute of truth and sincerity, as to cancel all his claims to our respect. His unscriptural views were condemned and speedily suppressed by the Church.

The doctrine of transubstantiation, which had gradually worked its way upward, and had first been fully developed and distinctly stated in the ninth century by Paschasius Rhadbertus,[8] was now, near the end of the eleventh century, the dominant view, having gained a complete victory over the heresy of Berengarius, and thrown into the background the original apostolic doctrine, which taught the real presence without defining the *quo modo* (the way in which this happens). As the power of the papal hierarchy increased, and more and more found its interest in perverting truth, superstition grew and spread and began to exert its baneful influence especially upon men's views of the Sacraments, of which there were (about A.D. 1100) assumed, without the slightest warrant from Scripture, to be seven. As respects the Eucharist, the doctrine of transubstantiation, (a term first used by Hildebert) which had, as we have seen, gradually gained the ascendancy, was first elevated into an article of faith by the fourth general Lateran Council, A.D. 1215 while Innocent III filled the papal see. It met with opposition from various quarters as late as the 13th century: especially from the theological faculty of Paris.

But soon every dissentient voice was hushed: papal bulls decreed the multiplication of superstitious practices and rites, and the *festum corporis Domani* (the feast of the body of Christ) capped the climax of the absurd and gorgeous mummeries of Rome. Even before the end of the 13th century the cup was denied to the laity. We have never learned how the introduction, by papal authority, of this unscriptural practice is to be reconciled with the pope's

---

1079: Alberic of Monte Cassino Against Berangar of Tours. (New York: Columbia, 2003)

[8] The essay of Radbertus as well as his opponent Ratramnus can be found in: McCracken, George E. and Allen Cabaniss. *Early Medieval Theology (The Library of Christian Classics IX).* (Philadelphia: Westminster, 1956), 90-153

alleged infallibility; for, as this departure from the original institution arose at first among heretics, Manichaeans, it was very rigorously condemned by several bishops of Rome. But the papacy is never at a loss for plausibilities.

Although the doctrine of transubstantiation was thus permanently incorporated, with all its associated absurdities, follies and abuses, in Rome's corrupt system, it did not enjoy its predominance unquestioned or unassailed for long. The original and purely scriptural doctrine of the Church began gradually to gain new friends and defenders, and to win its way to the respect and acceptance of candid inquirers. Durandus, a very eminent French divine (1332) d'Ailly, chancellor of the University of Paris, afterwards bishop of Cambray, and subsequently cardinal (1425) openly declared that the doctrine of transubstantiation was contrary to both Scripture and reason. Its prominent antagonist, however, was Wycliffe (1384) who unfortunately was not satisfied with rejecting the popish heresy, but proceeded to deny, as Berengarius and Ratramnus had done before him, that there was any real presence of the body and blood of Christ in the Eucharist.

The same denial appears in the writings of some other theologians of the period immediately preceding the Reformation; and thus it was reserved for Luther and the apologists and expounders of the Augsburg Confession, again distinctly to assert, clearly to unfold, and triumphantly to vindicate the pure doctrine of Scripture as taught in the words of the institution and in the 1st Epistle to the Corinthians, and held by the primitive Church.

Dr. Schmucker, in his Article on the Eucharist, cites indeed the language of the Augustana as quoted and explained by the Apology, and introduces (as he tells us, by way of explanation!) the word Romish bracketed into the language of the Apology. The Apology, both in the German and in the Latin language, distinctly mentions the Greek Church (or its Canon) as well as the Romish (in the German the Romish is not named, but evidently intended): and as the word hitherto occurs in the passage quoted, we should like to know what other churches than the Romish and the Greek the Apology could have referred to: we should like to be informed whether, during many centuries preceding the Reformation, the Church really was utterly extinct, or whether the Greek and Roman communions, however corrupt, were still to be regarded as Churches. If not, we should like to know at what precise period the Church became extinct: we suppose it must have expired immediately after the reputed conversion of Constantine the Great, for everybody knows that during his reign, and through his intervention, the flood of corruptions began to sweep over the Church. The language of the Apology, which Dr. Schmucker so skillfully cites, with his amendment or supplement in brackets, is perfectly proper and just, and cannot, as is there attempted, be employed against the Reformers.

When Luther first began to protest and contend against the corruptions of the Romish church, he was, as is well known, by no means prepared to reject the doctrine of transubstantiation, although even at this early period he was far more attentive to maintain that the Savior is really present in the Eucharist, than to explain the manner of this presence. It required a longer and more searching study of the Scriptures to lead him to a correct view of this great subject. In his subsequent contests against the Romish superstition, he could not fail to perceive that this would be most effectually disposed of, by assuming that the bread and wine were nothing more than symbolic signs. But he soon obtained the clear and full conviction, never again to be disturbed or shaken, that every exegesis which denies a real presence of the body of Christ in the sacred Supper, is utterly irreconcilable with the words of the institution, and the parallel passages. And adhering subsequently, with unwavering firmness to the position, that the body and blood of Christ are truly and really present in the Eucharist, he continued more clearly, soberly, considerately and intelligently to unfold, to divest of all human aides, and to illustrate the doctrine, on the basis of the Scriptures and the faith of the primitive Church, establishing it firmly in the dogmatic system of the Church, and at the same time, from the year 1520, he maintained that transubstantiation was a fiction of scholastic-metaphysical subtlety, while he more and more thoroughly demonstrated the real presence of the bread, as well as the body of Christ. In this view, Melanchthon entirely agreed in the first edition of his *loci*. That he afterwards changed his views and brought more than a little evil in the Church.

However, the discussions and controversies which subsequently arose in Germany around this doctrine do not concern us here. Although it passed through many modifications in the dogmatic systems of individual theologians and their disciples, the great body of the Church has always adhered to the pure doctrine of the Scriptures, as held by the early Christians, and fully exhibited in our symbolical books.

There is, however, one point of history which it is well to notice here. The American-Lutheran opponents of our symbolical (Confessional) theology are, probably to a man, great admirers of Spener:[9] in their estimation the pietistic development in the Lutheran Church of Germany formed the most thriving period, the *rue Bluthezeit*, of Lutheranism: whatever sympathies they may have with Lutheranism seem to revolve around this point as their center, or here to find their focus. It is well known that the leader and principal advocate of American Lutheranism is not a whit behind his school in this distinguished admiration of Spener and his measures. We too entertain a high regard for Spener's pure and lofty character, and profoundly admire his laborious and devoted efforts for the conversion of sinners and the advancement of vibrant piety.

---

[9] The founder of Lutheran pietism.

But although the views of practical religion which he held and avowed, and the measures which he adopted present some analogies to the views and operations of those who in this country practiced, or still practice, what has been called "new measures," yet, unlike the friends of new measures in our communion, Spener never for an instant faltered in his loyal attachment to the Confessions of our Church; and we, accordingly, claim him as a strictly consistent symbolic Lutheran. That we do not here speak unadvisedly, we consider it of some importance to demonstrate. We have before us the exposition of Christian Doctrine, published by Spener for the use of the German churches, under the title: *"Dr. Philipp Jacob Spener's einfache Erklaerung der christlichen Lehre nach der Ordnung des kleinen Latechismus Luthers in Fragen und Antworten verfasst und mit noethigen Zeugnissen der Schrift bewaehrt."* The only point which here concerns us is his position relative to our doctrine concerning the Lord's Supper. Here he first answers the question: "How do the papists understand these words (i.e. of the institution)?" in strong terms of disapproval, enforcing them with suitable reasons. Then on page 427 comes the question: "But how do the Reformed understand it (the Eucharist)?" This he answers thus:

> So as that the body and blood of Christ are, in their essential reality present only in heaven above, whilst on earth, on the other hand, nothing but bread and wine are present; that these are memorials of the body and blood of Christ, in the use of which faith recalls these to recollection, and therefore partakes of them in a spiritual and figurative manner." "Is this," he proceeds to ask, "the correct understanding?"

The answer is:

> No: this also cannot be the meaning of the Lord. For, 1. This view also is an artificial mode of dealing with the language of the Testament and the word 'is' is

defined to denote 'signifies'; 2. The Lord does not say, this is the memorial feast or the virtue of my body, but, this is my body; 3. The apostle calls the bread the communion of the body of Christ (1. Cor. 10:16), which must therefore be united with it; since, according to that (the Reformed) exposition, not the bread, but faith would be the communion of the body of Christ; 4. If, in the Holy Supper, we received Christ in no other way than merely by our faith, that Supper would have been instituted in vain and without any use, since this spiritual partaking of him takes place constantly, independently of the Holy Sacraments, which is not compatible with the wisdom of our Savior; 5. We would have nothing more in the Holy Sacrament than the worthy Ancients had in their paschal lamb with a much more palpable significance (a signification much more easily apprehended), seeing that they also, when eating it, became partakers, by faith, of the spiritual benefits obtained for us by Christ; and this would be contrary to the nature (Art) of both Testaments, because "in the Old we find the shadow, but in the new the reality of these benefits. (26-31)

Now comes the question: "What is the correct understanding of these words?" Which is thus answered:

That which our Church teaches in simplicity; to wit, that in the Holy Supper we truly receive bread, as we perceive by our taste, sight and smell; but that, at the same time, through the efficacy of the institution by Christ are truly presented to us, together with the bread, the real body of Christ, and, together with the wine, the real blood of Christ, to be partaken of by us, although of this we neither see nor taste anything.

Again he asks: "How are we assured that this is the correct understanding?" Answer:

> Because 1., This is the simplicity of the letter in the words of the institution, if we understand them, as we are accustomed, in common life, to understand such expressions as, 'this is an excellent medicine,' and the like; 2., Especially, because Paul calls the bread the communion of the body of Christ, 1 Cor. 10.16, whence bread and wine must be present, and connected in closest union; 3., it is inseparable from the nature of the Sacraments in which the earthly and the heavenly are wont always to be together, and united with each other. See p. 428.

He asks again: "But what manner of eating is it?" Answer:

> Not by any means a natural corporeal eating, for the natural nourishment of the body, as though the body of Christ were masticated, digested in the stomach, and converted into nutriment for our bodies: may all such thoughts be far from us; and yet it is real eating, so that with the bodily mouth we receive, and partake of, not only the bread and the wine, but also the body and the blood of the Lord, for the spiritual nourishment of our inward man, with which, in this food, Christ unites himself. See p. 429.

Again he asks: "In what manner does this eating and drinking take place?" Answer:

> This is incomprehensible to us, whence we are not to endeavor any further to search out what is not revealed to us, nor, on the other hand, to question the divine omnipotence and truth as to anything of which God assures us. But is it possible that Christ's body can be present and partaken of at so many places?

> How this is possible it is not necessary to understand;
> for it is a mystery which is above our comprehension,
> nevertheless we believe the word of Him who is the
> truth, and cannot lie. See p. 430.

That the patriarchs of the Church in America adhered
consistently and strictly to this evangelical doctrine, is
abundantly demonstrated by unquestionable evidence. The
first Lutheran Congregations in this country were established
on the basis of divine truth as confessionally exhibited in the
Augustana.[10] Through the operation of external influences,
chiefly Presbyterian, Puritan and Methodistic, the faith of the
Church became gradually unsettled and more and more
modified, her scriptural view of the Sacraments vitiated, and
eventually supplanted by Zwinglian notions, and her usages
neglected, and superseded by novel practices, so that, in the
progress of time, her doctrinal system and her ritual were
imperceptibly accommodated and conformed to the
confessions and usages of surrounding communions, and in
the end entirely metamorphosed. This new state of things, for
a long time irregular and chaotic, was after a while arranged
and organized, chiefly through the agency of the Lutheran
Observer and the Rev. Dr. Schmucher, into a mongrel
system, half Lutheran, half multifariously otherwise. But it
was not long before the leaders of this unchurchly
movement, after publishing their novel views in such works
as, "Why are you a Lutheran:" "Portraiture of Lutheranism:"
"Popular Theology," etc. finding that, notwithstanding their
efforts in behalf of "American Lutheranism," the consistent
adherents of the unaltered Augustana were greatly multiplying
in our land, turned from their first unspoken, then explicit
denials, and their zealous system-building, to open warfare
against the distinctive characteristics of genuine Lutheranism.
The Rev. Dr. Shmucker of the Gettysburg Seminary, who by

---

[10] See Muhlenberg's Journal, and *Hallische Nachrichten*

his own showing,[11] received and defended, at the beginning of his professorial career, the Lutheran doctrine of the Lord's Supper, after the effort to centralize "American Lutheranism" by means of the General Synod, in connecting himself actively with the effort when it was in danger of sinking, employed it, at a subsequent period, in support of his later views. After exerting himself to the utmost for the promulgation of these views, through the publication of various writings and the training of young minds, has at last stood forth for years, aided by his disciples and the Lutheran Observer, as the avowed enemy, the unrelenting antagonist of our Confessions.

But, in spite of all these arduous efforts, a mighty reaction against this unconfessional and unchurchly movement and system has of late years appeared. Thoughtful and candid minds, perceiving the irregularity, inconsistency and perils of our condition, grew weary and sick of the anomalous position of our Church in America. Earnest inquiry, a strong desire, produced by our pressing necessities, to possess a distinct and definite confession to cling to and avow before men, and to have an established and not ever tottering, a well ordered and not ever confused and distracted ecclesiastical home in which they may dwell in quietness and safety, have led back great numbers to the only known confessional basis of our Evangelical Church. This reaction has indeed intensified the energy and virulence of the antagonistic elements; but, in spite of all opposing efforts, the change for the better, the revolution in favor of our venerable standards, is growing and spreading apace. Thus only can our Church in American attain to unity, strength, and permanently vigorous vitality. May the Great Head of the Church preside over and guide this auspicious movement, and hasten on the day when all who bear the name of Lutheran shall rally, with united hearts and hands, around the

---

[11] See the first Ed. of his translation of Storr and Flatt's Theology

glorious standards of the first church of the Reformation, the one Evangelical Church.

CHAPTER 2
THE SCRIPTURAL CHARACTER OF THE LUTHERAN DOCTRINE OF THE LORD'S SUPPER

FOR a good many years past a great deal has been written, and in various ways published, by ministers in connection with the Lutheran Church in America, from which those without, and Christians of other denominations, can only draw one of two inferences: either that the Lutheran is a confessionless church; or that her confession is a dead letter—long since defunct and buried in oblivion, or at best existing only as a target to be shot at or as a starting point for all sorts of subjective speculations. Indeed, the most recent exhibitions, on the part of those who sustain this singular relation to our standards, which are really not yet quite declining, are calculated to produce the impression abroad, that there is nothing definite and fixed about Lutheranism. They say that Lutheranism is a vague abstraction, having no hold on men's minds or hearts; waiting to be rendered acceptable to this enlightened and progressive age, admitting and requiring indefinite development, in accordance with the liberal ideas, and expanding views of this highly intelligent and rapidly advancing generation. We have in recent years, seen one publication follow fast upon the other, calculated to produce this impression upon those who are not of our communion, and equally so upon many who worship in our sanctuaries, but who, from many causes not to be here investigated, are ignorant of the standards, the doctrines, principles and usages of the first Church of the Reformation, the church of their fathers. In vain do writers, whose efforts tend to create such impressions, allege that the system which they are advocating is genuine Lutheranism. The plea would be summarily ruled out of every court of justice, and scouted by every competent and impartial jury.

If Lutheranism is indeed a dogmatic system, susceptible of indefinite development in all sorts of subjective directions, then, truly, it would be time to renounce it as having no foundation on that eternal rock of truth, the Word of God: if it be indeed a shifting quicksand, never the same, but ever changing its shape and bearings, with every tide of human opinion sweeping over it who, could maintain his foothold on it? Who would venture to erect upon it the spiritual dwelling of his sojourn in this mortal state? But Lutheranism is no such baseless and unstable system—no such ever-varying, ever-shifting sandbank. We deplore deeply and bitterly these destructive efforts, not only because we fervently love the Church of our Fathers and feel the wrongs heaped upon her as though they were done to ourselves, but because we see but too plainly either all this naturally and necessarily tends; to the multiplication of controversies, to the destruction of harmony in feeling and action, to the increase and perpetuation of disunion, if not eventually of something still more earnestly to be condemned.

We have repeatedly intended and undertaken to discuss the subject named at the head of this article, and have refrained from carrying our purpose into effect, merely because we did not wish rashly and prematurely to provoke controversy, or to lay ourselves open to the ready charge of distracting the Church by an unnecessary tension of contested points. But silence on such points has ceased to be a virtue in those who are true to the doctrinal system of our Church. A war of extermination has long been carried on against the distinctive doctrinal views of our Church, leaving those who are not willing to see her standard pulled down and trodden in the dust, no alternative but to buckle on their armor, and to enter the lists. We dare not sit still, and composedly regard, with cowardly indifference, the unceasing assaults made upon the articles of our faith.

The second article of the Evangelical Review for April, 1851 presents a sad exhibition of hostility to our evangelical standards. The writer of that article here prominently displays his fixed aversion to the Lutheran view of the Lord's Supper, as set forth in the Augustana and the subsequent Symbolical Books. Although we earnestly hope that more able pens than ours will undertake the defense of this so stubbornly contested view, we are impelled, by a sense of duty, to say something in vindication of a doctrine which we hold sacred and precious; but ere we proceed to the direct discussion of the subject itself, we would yet premise a few remarks with reference to an assertion made in that same article just specified Dr. S. there asserts, that Luther had parted from the doctrine of "the ubiquity or omnipresence of Christ's body, and that therefore he was himself no symbolic Lutheran." For this assertion no authority is given. Now we frankly acknowledge that we are utterly ignorant of any other foundation for this allegation, than the well-known fact that, at the Marburg colloquium, in his desire to promote or preserve the peace of the Church, Luther did at one time concede that Christ's body was circumscribed, whilst all who know this fact, also know, that the concession was retracted almost as soon as made, as a measure of compromise incompatible with his honest convictions. So much for Luther's being no symbolic Lutheran. But if this assertion be based upon the story so oft repeated and only recently again reiterated in Henry's Life of Calvin, that Luther had, shortly before his death, changed his view of the Lord's Supper, we have only to say, that this has not the slightest historical foundation, and is utterly and notoriously false. He is, indeed, reported to have, a short time before his death, admitted that he might have gone to too great lengths in his disputes concerning the Lord's Supper, in the severity with which he treated his opponents; but he nowhere says that his own views had undergone a change.

In the above-mentioned article of Dr. S. a good deal is said about Luther's protesting "against the practice of designating the Church of the Reformation by his name," and "against investing his writings with binding authority on his successors." But of these protests an improper use is here made. So far as the first point is concerned, the title: "Church of the Augsburg Confession," is quite acceptable, and in some paces nearly as current, as that of "the Lutheran Church:" in Hungary indeed, the former is the only title allowed by government to be used. And as respects the second particular, the Doctor knows very well, that Luther's protest has reference only to his private writings, and not to those which had, by special command, and with the aid of other learned and godly men, been drawn up for the benefit of the Church, for the establishment and defense, the exhibition and diffusion of her faith. That with these Melanchthon was only too much disposed to tamper, is well known, so that Luther one day seriously reproved him for it, adding that these writings were not private property, as they belonged to the Church, which had received and owned them as the exponents of her faith.

But, we proceed to the subject more immediately in hand, the real presence of our Savior's glorified humanity in the sacrament of the Lord's Supper; a doctrine which, together with those with which it is most intimately connected, stands, as we shall have occasion incidentally to show, in the most momentous and vital relation to the doctrine of the atonement. Dr. Schmucker gives, on p. 248, of his Popular Theology, what he considers a correct statement of the Lutheran view of this subject. That his statement is imperfect, every symbolic Lutheran will perceive at a glance. But we accept it for the present, as sufficiently accurate and explicit upon the point which here more particularly claims our attention, and as presenting in itself a satisfactory answer to sundry idle objections frequently made to the doctrine. His words are as follows:

> The bread and wine remain in all respects unchanged; but the invisible, glorified body and blood of Christ are also actually present at the celebration of the Eucharist, and exert an influence on all those who receive the bread and wine; not indeed present in that form nor with those properties which belonged to the Savior's body on earth, such as visibility, tangibility, etc., for these it no longer possesses, but with the new and elevated properties which now belong to its glorified state.

Although we may, ere we conclude, in just a few words, give what we conceive to be a just exhibition of the view taken by the Church, from the earliest times, of the Sacred Supper, and now held by the Lutheran Church, our present business is, to notice and briefly to answer many objections, which, though a hundred times refuted, are again and again brought forward, with as much confidence as if they were perfectly valid and unanswerable.

CHAPTER 3
FIGURATIVE LANGUAGE AND THE WORDS OF INSTITUTION

We begin with a few observations upon what will, of course, not be denied;[12] viz.: that the view of the Eucharist which, though found in the writings of the earliest Fathers, it is now unusual to designate as the Lutheran, is based upon the literal interpretation of the words of institution. Those who deny the correctness of this view maintain that our Savior's words are to be regarded as figurative. And we are accustomed to see it confidently affirmed, that the expressions employed by the Savior, in instituting this most solemn ordinance, come under the same category as these: "I am the door," "I am the vine," "I am the good Shepherd," etc. etc. To this view of the subject, there are many serious objections: we shall state only a few. And first, the instances just cited, and many others of the same character, occur in discourses in which our Savior was communicating important instruction, and illustrating truth, in that parabolic or highly figurative mode of

---

[12] This is denied by Dr. Schmucker, in the article which we received after this was written, and which is hereinafter answered: he calls Luther's "The first figurative interpretation."

expression, which he so often adopted; and in these instances there was no danger of his being misunderstood. But on the occasion of his last solemn passover with his disciples, he was not teaching, not communicating instruction, in no sense of the word preaching, but he was appointing a sacred rite, instituting, for all coming time, the most holy of Christian ordinances; an occasion therefore on which, it strikes us, figurative language would have been singularly out of place. We trust that we are not presumptuous in supposing, that our Lord would, in a transaction like the present, most earnestly and solicitously seek to avoid using any language capable of the least misconception, or misconstruction, (except it were willfull), and therefore free from the slightest ambiguity. We are, of course, not authorized to judge what was, or what was not, proper to be said or done by our Lord; but, at the same time, we are not to put constructions on his words, which, departing from their literal meaning, their direct and plain sense, are irreconcilable with that perfect wisdom which characterized all his proceedings. And we are compelled by common sense, and by our reverence for Him who "spoke as never man spoke," to regard the present occasion as one which preeminently demanded the utmost definiteness, or precision of language; so that if he should be thereafter misunderstood or misinterpreted, it could only be by rejecting the simple, literal meaning of his words, by distorting his language, and putting upon it an arbitrary and unwarranted construction.

If the Church has been distracted and divided by controversies respecting the nature of the Holy Supper, let its Holy Founder not be made responsible for these lamentable results, by representing his direct and simple language as being so infelicitous, so obscurely figurative, as naturally and necessarily to give rise to conflicting views. Take him as he speaks, and the whole difficulty vanishes. It is well known, that here was Luther's strongest foothold, in all his discussions and controversies concerning this important subject. He could never be induced to depart one hair's breadth form the only construction of which, according to the simplest principles of interpretation, our Savior's words will admit; because, as he declared, the text was too stringent, and left him no choice.

But again: the instances referred to, and so often cited as coming under the same category, and as showing how the words of the institution are to be understood, are not by any means parallel. It is contended that the words, "this is my body," "this is my blood," are to be thus explained: "this denotes or signifies my body," etc. If this be correct, and if the words of institution be in the same manner figurative as those figurative expressions which have been quoted, then it will be proper to construe these in the same way in which it is proposed to construe the words before us, thus: I signify the door: I signify the vine, I signify the light of the world: I signify the good shepherd. It needs not that we should labor to show how preposterous this would be.

There is nothing more easy, nothing that men are more ready to do, in explaining passages of Scripture that do not accord with their notions and theories, than to set up the plea that the language is figurative. It is in this way that Unitarians get rid of the Divinity of Christ: they hold the language of Scripture bearing upon this point to be strongly metaphorical, or, more strictly speaking, that figure of speech termed hyperbole, and denoting no more than a very eminent degree of that divinity, which they ascribe to mankind in general. It is well known, that in this way also the Universalists get rid of the doctrine of future and eternal punishments. We need not cite any more instances to show how cautious we ought to be in accepting such explanations, and how dangerous it is to apply the figurative theory, except in cases where the language is so palpably metaphorical, that it is impossible to understand it in any other way. That the words employed by our Savior in instituting the Sacrament of his Supper, present a case of this kind, has never yet been shown to the satisfaction of more than one-fourth of Christendom; and until those, who maintain that the language here is figurative, advance better reasons in support of their theory that we have yet seen, we must persist in peremptorily rejecting it. In the case of the Popish doctrine of transubstantiation the thing is perfectly clear, because here certain substances which are obviously one thing, are represented to be actually quite another thing. But with this absurdity the Lutheran view of the real presence of Christ's glorified humanity has evidently no connection whatever.

We know very well that Papists, who, though they imagine that they are most literal in their interpretation, are not so at all in reality, have been obliged to admit, that the cup is used figuratively for its contents. According to their view of the whole subject, this admission was unavoidable: but according to the Lutheran view it is perfectly immaterial whether we adopt it or not, because we do not believe in any transmutation or transubstantiation at all. And to our real view of this subject we are constrained to call the reader's particular attention, because writers on the opposite side are wont studiously to conceal it, or to express themselves in such a manner as to create the impression, that we are all but papistical transubstationists. We hold that it is in the Sacrament itself, in the solemn celebration of this sacred ordinance, that Christians enjoy the actual presence of the glorified Redeemer, and that the unchanged bread and wine, received by the communicant, are not only the outward visible signs of an inward spiritual grace; but, connected with the word and promise of God, the vehicles through whose instrumentality the divine Savior communicates himself to those who partake of them. Hence the real presence of Christ in the Eucharist, as believed by Lutherans, is frequently designed as a "sacramental presence." That this view is founded on a far more literal interpretation of the words of the institution, one philologically more correct, than is that of the Papists, it is not difficult to show. Luther himself very well knew what an advantage he had here; and he did not fail to make good use of it, treating with merited indignation and scorn Carlstadt's perversions of the grammatical structure of the sentences containing the words of institution.

The point, which we have here particularly in view, is this. The English version of the N.T. reads thus: "This is my body:" "This is my blood of the New Testament," etc. The translation is perfectly correct; but, as the demonstrative has in English no gender, it leaves room for a misapprehension, which might be avoided by circumlocution. As we have reason to look for the utmost precision in the words employed on the occasion of such an institution, the fact that our Lord does not say "this is the bread,"(ὁυτοζ ὁ ἀϱτοζ) or this bread is my body, is certainly not to be considered as accidental or unimportant. And when he says: "this is my body" (τουτό ἐστιν το σωμά μου), and "this is my blood" (τουτα γάϱ ἐστιν το αἱμα μου), we are by no means satisfied that this is merely because it is unusual in all languages to use the demonstrative in the neuter gender, in pointing to an object that is directly before us, and concerning which we are about to say something. We conceive the τουτό (this) to be used with wise design, in calling the attention of his disciples to that which is bestowed upon them, in the act of giving them the bread: to the sacramental gift bestowed in connection with, and instrumentally through, the gift of the bread. Bengel's exposition of the words, which accords with this view, and embodies it, has met with general acceptance: *Hoc quod vos sumere jubeo* (This thing which I command you to take). etc. And this vigilant caution of the Savior to guard against misapprehension, appears still more plainly in his not afterwards saying: ὁυτος ὁ οιναζ (this the wine), etc. but, if the words of Luke should be preferred as the most full and precise: "τουτο τὸ ποτήϱιον ἡ καινή"(this cup of the new) etc. That ποτήϱιον (cup) is here employed figuratively for its contents, does not, as we have already remarked, concern us at all, as it does not affect our position in the least; for we are not defending the transubstantiation of Papists, but the mysterious, sacramental presence taught in accordance with Scripture, by the Lutheran Church, which believes the Savior to say: That which I give you in presenting you this cup, that which ye receive in drinking its contents, is my blood, is the fullness of the blessing of the New Testament (covenant) in my blood.

Again, the Sacred Supper of the New Covenant has come, with all its substantial realities, into the place of the passover under the Old. The passover stood in a peculiar and mysterious relation to a great historical event, which it afterwards symbolically shadowed forth, and commemorated. The event itself was typical of the greater deliverance which we owe to Christ out passover, sacrificed for us; and the celebration of the passover pointed to that sacred institution, in which believers feast sacramentally, in a manner mysterious and inexplicable, upon the body broken and the blood shed for the salvation of their souls. In the passover we have the shadow, in the Eucharist the reality; and this same typical relation of the former to the latter justifies the view which we take, viz. that the τουτο (this) is to be understood to mean: this which I now give you; or: this which I now appoint and institute to be partaken by you, and all who shall believe through your word. If we reject this view of the subject, we lose the actual, positive, objective reality of the Christian Sacrament, as distinguished from the typical rite of the old covenant.

Not to prolong too much of our discussion, we will only add, that the passages which are so confidently appealed to as illustrating, and even proving, the figurative character of our Savior's language in instituting his Holy Supper, are in yet another respect unsatisfactory: they are figurative only in a very modified and limited sense: expressions which would apply in a very narrow, and in a highly metaphorical sense to ordinary human beings, are applicable to him with a breadth and comprehensiveness of scope, with a reality, depth, height, and force of meaning, which they but faintly express. Thus it is a strong metaphor to say, that a distinguished statesman is the pillar of the state, or that some gifted politician is the soul of his party. But, on the other hand, when Christ calls himself the light of the world, the way and the truth and the life, the door, the vine, the good shepherd, etc. there is a vast and unsearchable and unfigurative reality in these representations, which means that they are not metaphors in the broadest sense. He is the religious and moral light of the world, its central and only Sun: there is no door or way of access to God but himself, and through him, actually and exclusively, we come to the Father: He is the truth, its impersonation, embodiment, and essence; and whatsoever in the religious and moral world does not emanate from him, point and lead to him, is not truth: He is life, it's very author, source and fullness, and out of him there is no life; nothing but death dark and dismal.

We do not need to dwell on other instances, showing that even where the language used by the Savior of himself, may, in a certain limited sense, be regarded as figurative, the words have a literal force of reality, which the loftiest figures, into which the boldest fancy could mold human language, cannot adequately describe: and if so, how idle is it to talk of figurative language in connection with that solemn institution, into which the obscurity of metaphor can only introduce inextricable confusion, as the writings of all who adopt the figurative theory so amply and lamentably prove. Taking the personage who spoke, and the occasion on which he spoke, together, we conceive all figurative language to be utterly and totally out of the question.

The next objection made to our view of the Eucharist, which we would briefly notice, is, that it is a new doctrine—a doctrine invented in later times. That the Popish doctrine of transubstantiation is comparatively modern; that, indeed, it did not assume its present form, until it was, in the ninth century, distinctly thus stated by Paschasius Rhadbertus, is undoubtedly true: evidence of its having been rejected by the early Fathers can be found collected, in ample detail, in Bishop Burnet's Exposition of the Thirty Nine Articles. But what have Lutherans to do with this Popish dogma?

We notice it in this connection only, because those who oppose the Lutheran doctrine concerning the Sacrament, are, from motives best known to themselves, perpetually dragging the absurdities of Papistry into their discussions, and bringing them into some sort of connection with the views set forth in our Confession. We might as well bring in and belabor the doctrines of Zerduscht or Kongfutse, for the purpose of casting disgust upon the Anxious Bench. That the doctrine concerning the Lord's Supper, which is held by the Lutheran Church is modern—that it was either not known, or offensive, to the early Church, is not true; and although, as we have on a former occasion distinctly declared, we do not ascribe to the Fathers any authority to define and settle, for all subsequent ages, the doctrine of the Church, we regard, and must regard and believe them, as competent and true witnesses concerning the common faith and practice of the primitive Church. But on the entire point here at issue we do not intend to expatiate at any length: we shall content ourselves with translating the following short passage from Stier's Commentary on the Discourses of our Lord, Vol. VI. p. 161:

> The testimony of the Fathers, from Ignatius, Justin, and Irenaeus downward, is known to the learned. In opposition to the opinions of heretics the ὁμολογεῖν [unanimous testimony, TR.] of the Church is clear and decided: τὴν εὐχαρισίαν σάρχα εἶναι τοῦ σωτηρος ἡμῶν παρουσαν, ἣν τῃ χρεσότετι ὁ πατήρ ἠγειρεν.[13] They know and confidently testify: "Ου γὰρ 'ὡς κοίνον 'αρτον ὀυδέ κοινόν πόμα ταῦτα λαμβάνομεν ἐκείνου τοῦ σαρχοποιηθεντῖος Ἰησοῦ καὶ σάρκα καὶ αἷμα ἐδιδαχθημεν εἶναι.[14] To explain away this κοινή

---

[13] "That the Eucharist is the flesh of our Savior Jesus Christ, which suffered for our sins, and which, through his goodness, the Father raised"--i.e. from the dead.

[14] "We do not receive these as common bread or a common drink--we have been taught that they are both the flesh and the blood of that same

πίστισ (common faith) of the Church from the beginning, is sophistry; and to contradict it, from a conceit of superior wisdom, is, for that very reason, at least suspicious."

On a subject of this kind we do not consider the speculations of modern theologians, however vastly learned or wonderfully enlightened, worth anything, in comparison with the doctrinal views of those who lived and wrote in the age immediately succeeding that of the apostles, from whom their knowledge of Christian doctrine was directly derived.

Jesus who was made flesh."

By this the early Fathers meant no such thing as transubstantiation. We have already stated where a great number of citations from their writings may be found collected, showing that they repudiated the doctrine which the Romish Church afterwards embraced. They could then have held none other than the Lutheran view.

CHAPTER 4
THE REAL PRESENCE AND HUMAN REASON

WE proceed to examine now, as briefly as possible, an argument which is constantly used, and very much relied upon, as quite conclusive against the doctrine of our Confessions concerning the Sacrament of the Lord's Supper. This doctrine, it is contended, is contrary to all experience, and utterly at variance with the laws of matter—the laws which govern bodily existences, and confine each distinct body to some particular space or locality. With respect to the first point, the seeming tension between our doctrine and human experience, we do not think it is worthwhile to say much. Every well-educated man knows that this is Hume's argument against our Lord's miracles—against the possibility of miracles. The futility of his premises or general principles has been demonstrated, and the rottenness of his argument fully exposed, in a variety of dissertations written by grave and able men; and archbishop Whately has effectually exposed his fallacies, and held them up to the ridicule and scorn which they deserve, in his celebrated work entitled "Historic Doubts relative to Napoleon Bonaparte." Theologians had better be careful how they avail themselves of modes of reasoning adopted by infidels, when they seek to discredit doctrines, which a great part of Christendom find in the Scriptures, but which are irreconcilable with their subjective views—their own theories. For the past experience of mankind we could care less when it comes in conflict with anything revealed in the word of Him who has made all things, and knows all things.

To this argument about human experience, the attitude of the present age is not very favorable; for the discoveries in physical science, and the countless inventions in all the mechanical arts, which have, for many years past, been astonishing and revolutionizing the world, have long since turned all implicit reliance upon the past experience of mankind most unceremoniously out of doors; and there we shall leave it, to be condoled with by those who regard it with sympathy.

But the other point deserves a more extended notice, though we do not think it will be difficult to show, that it has no greater value than the one which we have just considered. There is then, no objection more frequently and confidently urged against the Lutheran view of the Eucharist than this: that it contradicts the evidence of our senses, and the universal observation of mankind, by which it is fully ascertained, that a body cannot be in more than one place at a time. Now, that this is entirely true, and that this objection is perfectly valid, in respect of the ordinary bodies or substances belonging to this terrestrial globe, this temporal, mundane economy, is unhesitatingly admitted; although there are even here, as we shall see, some startling phenomena not a little perplexing to positive generalizers. Nor do we doubt that bodies or substances, such as we are conversant with, are subject to the same law, in whatever part of God's universe they may be found. But this does not prove that there may not be corporeal, substantial existences of a much higher order, and subject to far other laws, than those which come under our observation. It seems to us in the last degree brash and presumptuous for the occupants of this little globe, this speck in the vast universe, confidently to assert that the laws which govern their existence, and the position and movements of the bodies which surround them, must be the same throughout the immeasurable realms of creation.

It is perfectly clear from Scripture that angelic beings either have bodies, or have often assumed them for special purposes; and all (we believe without exception) the angelic appearances related in the Bible clearly prove that the laws which govern their presence and movements are totally different from those to which we are subject. And, in view of all this, it certainly does not become us to assert that, in devising and ordaining the order of things prevailing on earth, or throughout our solar system, the Almighty has exhausted his power of invention and design. It would be preposterous arrogance to assert, that other regions of the universe may not be subject to physical laws, the very reverse of those which prevail on our sphere of action. And although all this is mere speculation, it is, at all events, evident that to elevate the evidence of our senses, or universal human observation into a universal law for the entire creation, is nonsense; especially when we are certain that beings belonging to a higher economy, and coming frequently, perhaps being constantly, in contact with human affairs, obey far other laws than those which govern the grosser elements of our nature.

But letting all this pass, we remark again, that the evidence of our senses, or the universal observation of mankind, is trustworthy and valuable only as far as it goes, which, in some directions, is certainly not very far. For all the ordinary practical purposes of life its availability is perfect, and its value inappreciable. But let it be considered, that even within the sphere of daily inspection and inquiry it encounters mysteries, which are as utterly inexplicable as the doctrine which we are discussing. Let it be remembered, that in numberless instances, the evidence of our senses, or the universal observation of mankind, bears witness only of undeniable facts, whose rationale is certain, whose mode of being to discover and define, is utterly beyond the reach of human capacity. There are facts in natural history and chemistry, which, however clearly ascertained as facts, no human intellect can, or ever will understand or explain, except perhaps, amid the light of the future world. And some of these are isolated things, standing solitary and alone, having no analogies in the wide compass of nature, defying our senses to discover anything like them anywhere else, appealing to universal observation for their utter singularity, flatly contradicting all collateral experience, and refusing to bestow upon the acutest sagacity, and the keenest scrutiny, even the minutest spark of in formation respecting their real nature, or mode of being. And do we therefore ever dream of denying such facts?

We refuse to employ the sophistry which is so common in discussions of this kind. Let it not, therefore, be supposed, that we are urging these considerations with the design of producing anywhere the impression that they have any direct bearing upon the great subject of the present treatise. We present them merely in order to show that the appeal to our senses, and the universal observation of mankind must go for nothing in a case which lies confessedly beyond the scope of our senses, and could not be searched out, if all the power of observation possessed by the whole human race were concentrated into one intensely keen and piercingly scrutinizing gaze; while, on the other hand, even the common material world offers to our inspection countless facts and phenomena of extraordinary interest, the real nature of which our senses strive in vain to penetrate and ascertain. And here we wish to enter our solemn protest against the practice so often resorted to, of applying the so-called laws of nature, or of matter, to facts or doctrines revealed in the Word of God respecting a higher economy than ours, and then determining, according to these laws, (in other words, according to the evidence of our senses, or of universal observation), in what manner these facts or doctrines are to be explained.

What, we would ask, are the laws of nature or of matter? Are they unalterable statutes imposed by nature (who is nature?) upon herself? Are they laws, evolved by matter out of itself, and determining the nature or mode of its existence and its movements, with a precision and a stringency that admit of no exceptions or as a shadow of existence, independent of the will, of the originating and sustaining power of Him who alone did and could ordain them? If he should will their discontinuance or abolition; indeed, if he ceased to will that they shall continue to exist and to operate, would they not instantaneously cease to be, as utterly as if they had never been? And can He not then change or annihilate them at his pleasure? Or are they green vines, with which the Almighty Creator has so completely tied up his own hands, that he cannot move, or control at pleasure, his own works? When our Savior, while on earth, healed diseases with a touch or a word, nay, at a distance probably of miles from those upon whom his power was exerted, how much of the process was submitted to the senses of those around him? Did they see anything more than an effect? Had they not, up to that time, the most decided evidence of their senses, and of universal observation, that diseases and those the most frightful, are not healed by a touch or a word? And when with a word he raised the dead, did they not unanimously testify, that such a thing had never been seen or heard of before?

We repeat, that we advance these considerations merely in order to insist, that when the Almighty chooses to adopt some mode of procedure different from any ever witnessed before, and in which our senses shall be completely at fault; when it is his pleasure that Moses shall see a bush obviously burning and yet not burning; when it pleases him to go against all the past experience and observation of men; when the disciples can walk all the way to Emmaus with Jesus, and sit at meat with him, and yet not know him, though they had known him for years, it is all folly and presumption to say that these things cannot and must not be because they contradict the evidence of men's senses, and universal observation.[15] And if thus it is folly and impertinence to assert, in a general way, that God shall do nothing, and reveal nothing, or that no interpretation of his word shall stand, that does not accord with the evidence of our senses as if these were infallible and could not be deceived, or that does not correspond with the past universal observation of mankind, how much more rude and arrogant is it to apply this principle to a doctrine which has reference to a glorified body, mysteriously and inseparably united with an infinitely glorious divine nature, and when we know nothing of the capabilities of a glorified body, least of all of a glorified body united, like our Savior's, with the divine nature of the Son of God.

But for the further discussion of this point we are not yet ready. For the present we wish to show, that even with reference to our Savior's humanity, previous to his being glorified, it is unacceptable to reason from the universal observation and experience of mankind. We contend, that

---

[15] Dr. Schmucker says, in his Article on the Nature of the Savior's Presence in the Eucharist, p. 38, Ev. Rev. for July, 1851:

"No testimony is so strong as that of the senses; because on it rests our belief even of the Scriptures." This assertion calls for important qualifications. The testimony of the senses is so sure as to be safely relied upon in all the ordinary affairs, and common practical interests of life. But it is reliable only when the sense observe under favorable circumstances: when the object seen is near, and in a clear light : when the sound heard is distinct, and when the object from which it proceeds; is seen, or, at least, certainly known to be the only one in the place capable of producing it. But our senses are so notoriously subject to a great many illusions, that the fact has been, long since, put into the form of a proverb : as, "Der Scheintriigt :" — "Appearances are deceitful."

What becomes of the evidence of the senses, as respects the feats performed by modern Hindu and Egyptian magicians, by such jugglers as Blitz and Anderson, and by many so-called ventriloquists? What is the origin of most ghost stories? When Dr. Webster was under trial, two very respectable women testified under oath, that they had seen Dr. Parkman after the time of his alleged murder. Everybody knows that our senses are liable to be deceived in numberless ways.

various important events in the history of our Lord's earthly life forbid us to apply to his person the ordinary laws of matter, or to erect them into barriers to his movements and activity, when, in his infinite wisdom, he sees fit to disregard what is no doubt the ordinary course of things, and to dissolve relations which, though ascertained to prevail as far as we know, in general, we have no authority to consider as imperative laws, by which the Creator himself, (and is not the Son of God the Creator)? had literally tied his own hands. On one occasion, Christ was seen walking on the sea, and even enabled Peter to do the same so long as he believed. What became here, in the persons of Peter and the Lord, of the laws of matter? Was the law of gravitation suspended, or was the water congealed, or were their bodies sublimated into something lighter than water? The answer is due from those who reject the doctrine of the real presence, because it conflicts with the known and established laws of matter or corporeity. Thus also our Lord seems, after his resurrection, to have appeared to his disciples in different forms (see Mark 16:12.); and on one occasion, as related by Luke (24:36) and John (20:19), he suddenly stood in their midst, when, for fear of the Jews, the doors were shut, or rather, locked—bolted, barred, secured, fastened. Were the well-known laws of matter or corporeity observed on these occasions?

But again, at the marriage in Cana the Lord turned a great quantity of water into wine, so that, in defiance of the evidence of the senses of those who had poured the water into the vessels, the space just occupied by the water was now full of wine. On another occasion lie fed four thousand men, besides women and children, with what to their senses was obviously nothing more than five loaves and two fishes, and yet there were afterwards twelve baskets full of broken meat taken up. At another time he fed about four thousand persons, with what no mortal senses could make out to be more than seven loaves and a few small fishes, and afterwards seven baskets full of broken meat were taken up. It may be objected to these instances, that they were miracles. So doubtless they were: but what, then, are miracles?

The question, however, here is, what became then, whatever becomes of the well-known and established laws of matter or corporeity as applied to Christ's person and activity? In the last two instances mentioned it may be urged, that there was an exercise of creative power put forth in the production of the more that was needed in addition to what was on hand. The explanation may be correct: we do not profess to know or understand, when "God moves in a mysterious way." All that we do know about it is what our Lord himself afterwards said to his disciples respecting these two events, when they were indulging in unprofitable surmises: "Do you not remember? When I broke the five loaves among five thousand, how many baskets full of fragments took ye up? And when the seven among Jour thousand, how many baskets full of fragments took ye up?" Mark 8:19-20.

We once more repeat that we do not bring forward these remarkable and wonderful occurrences, to which others might be added, because we regard them as having any direct connection with the subject here under consideration, but because they prove that to oppose the laws of matter to the Lutheran doctrine of the real presence of Christ's glorified humanity in the Lord's Supper amounts to nothing; that it will not do to apply the ordinary laws of matter or corporeity to the glorified humanity of Him, who, while on earth, was subject to these laws no further than it pleased him and the Father that he should be. If the doctrine of transubstantiation involves an absurdity or impossibility, it would obviously be carrying human presumption entirely too far, to affirm the same of the view of the Lord's Supper inculcated in Scripture, held by the early Church, and set forth in our Confessions.

CHAPTER 5
THE WORDS OF INSTITUTION AND CHRIST'S GLORIFIED BODY

THUS far we had written, when Dr. Schmucker's article in the last number of this Review having come to hand, we glanced our eye over its pages. The obvious necessity of replying to this production will give to the present article a form entirely different from what we had intended. So we do not have to keep arguing the same point, we shall proceed briefly to discuss the point which, in our original plan came next in order. The objection we refer to here has been brought forward time and again, but as Dr. S. states it anew with undiminished confidence, we shall refer the reader to his remarks, which we do not have the space to quote in full.[16] The sum and substance of the objection is, that the Lutheran "interpretation" of the words of institution:

> Cannot be correct, because the glorified body, which is said to be received with the elements, had actually not yet any existence, and therefore could not have

---

[16] They will be found on page 42 under c, d, and e.

been given by the Savior to his disciples at the Holy Supper; that the Eucharist could not have conferred the broken body to the disciples at its institution, because it was not yet broken, & that the old Lutheran theory cannot be correct, according to the language of Christ; because he says, Luke 22:19. "Do this in remembrance of me"

The amount of this formidable objection is just this, that, if the Eucharist be what we Lutherans believe and say it is, then the disciples did not, at the time of the institution, receive it actually, in its real nature, and in the fullness of its power and blessing, and that hence the Lord's Supper, as celebrated subsequently to our Lord's ascension and glorification, is totally different from what it was at the institution.

We shall presently show that it is perfectly competent and safe for us to take this position ourselves. But before we explain ourselves on this particular point, there is another, the third above stated, which must he noticed. The three objections to which we have just referred constitute, in fact, the three links of one connected chain of argument; and it is only strange that those, who use this argument against the Lutheran interpretation of the words of institution, do not see that, if it proves anything at all, it proves entirely too much for their purpose. If the Lutheran doctrine is wrong, because the Eucharist could not at its institution be what it is now claimed to be, inasmuch as the Savior was then reclining, in his ordinary humanity, under the very eyes of his disciples, do not those who thus argue, discern, that this very same reasoning annihilates their own view of the Lord's Supper ? It is to them a commemorative ordinance, very little, if anything, more, so far as we can discover. If it is this, it has, of course, ever since the events which it commemorates, been entirely different from what it was at the time of institution; for how could it, at that time, commemorate what was yet future: our Lord's last sufferings and death?

To the opponents of the Lutheran doctrine, this argument is therefore worse than useless for their purpose: if the Eucharist must have been, at the time of institution, what it now is, their reasoning reduces their sacramental supper to an unmeaning ceremony—a positive farce. Now it is very strange that Dr. S., who very clearly perceives this state of the case, and gives up entirely[17] the view that the Eucharist, in its commemorative character, was at the time of institution what it afterwards was and now is, does not perceive, that he renounces all right and title to the argument which he advances.[18] If it was not, at the time of .institution, commemorative, because the facts to be commemorated had not yet occurred, then, is it consistent with truth and justice to condemn the Lutheran doctrine, because, for the same reason, the Eucharist could not then have bestowed what we maintain it was designed to bestow, and does confer, after and since the crucifixion, ascension and glorification?

We shall, we hope, be forgiven for unfolding our view of the whole of this subject a little more fully. We regard it as perfectly clear and indisputable, that to the disciples the Eucharist could not, at its institution, have been what it subsequently was to the Church, the actual communion of the body and blood of Christ. This is not only because the Savior had not yet suffered and died, but for this reason also, that at that time they were evidently still entirely incapable of understanding him. Notwithstanding his discourse recorded in the sixth chapter of John's Gospel, by which the Lord obviously sought to prepare their minds for the institution of his Holy Supper and for just views of its nature. Also not withstanding his repeated declarations, that he was about to suffer and to die, it is entirely clear, not only from the manner in which they are described as having repeatedly expressed themselves in reply to such declarations, but from their whole conduct up to the time when they could no longer doubt that

---

[17] Page 43. e., and on subsequent pages.
[18] on page 42., c. and d.

he was risen again, that they had never fairly comprehended the nature, or duly appreciated the design of his mission; that they had utterly failed to understand what he had come to accomplish, and how his purpose was to be accomplished. Full of the unwarranted Messianic expectations of the Jews, they were persuaded, up to the moment when he was seized by the emissaries of the chief priests and elders, that he would throw off what they seem to have regarded as a disguise, and, placing himself at the head of the people, fulfill those political hopes which the Jewish nation connected with the coming of the Messiah. But when he was arrested by his enemies, they were overwhelmed with disappointment, and, filled with fear and dismay, "then all the disciples forsook him and fled." Before this event they had eaten the passover with their Master. And is it not perfectly clear, that under such circumstances, while they entertained such views and feelings and hopes, the Eucharist could not have had for them any intelligible present meaning and significance? We cannot conceive it possible that they should have discerned, at the time, it's true import and design. For this reason, therefore, as well as for this, that their Master's body had not yet been scourged, and nailed to the cross, and pierced with the spear, the Eucharist could not, at the time of institution, have been what it afterwards became, and has been ever since to the Church, in whatever peculiar light it may be regarded; whether received front the Lutheran, the Calvinistic, or the Zwinglian standpoint. We may regard the whole transaction as prospective. The words used by the Savior as indicating the nature and design of the institution, and the entire action, and on his part that of the disciples, and presenting a normal type of the mode which the Eucharist was to be celebrated from that point forward.

We find the same view advanced by Stier who very properly urges that the case is the same as that of the Passover in Exodus 12, where the Exodus is spoken of as if it had already taken place. A similar instance of prospective language and even prospective action is found in John 20:22.

The disciples did not really receive the Spirit until long after this occurrence. All of these occurrences tend to render the manifest foolishness and dishonesty of every attempt to prove from this particular circumstance under which the Lord's Supper was instituted that it cannot be now what it could have been then. This view of the subject we have long held and have found it to be satisfactory. And yet the question sometimes comes up, whether it is giving too much to human reason. And when we consider this Holy Sacrament that it has a distinctive objective character of its own, independent of one's views respecting it, and that in the Savior there is so much which contradicts that which we assume to be true, so we must be willing to allow that the Holy Supper was mysteriously, yet truly and actually the body and blood of the lamb slain before the foundation of the world. While either view would be consistent with our Confessions, we would be strongly inclined to agree with the latter.

It had been our intention to carry out our discussion without direct reference to any writers who are opposed to the Lutheran Confessions. However, as the repeated rejections of those who disagree with our view of the Eucharist have been presented, in martial array, in Dr. Schmucker's recent article, it will, for various reasons, be best that we should take them up in the form, if not quite in the or der, in which they are there exhibited. And this we shall accordingly proceed to do.

There is but one point in the Doctor's Introduction which we feel called upon to notice. Respecting the doctrine here before us he states that:

> It has been a bone of contention in the Protestant Church, with but little intermission, ever since its origin, until about fifty years ago, when the Lutheran Church almost universally abandoned the views,

which Luther and his co-laborers, with few exceptions, entertained.[19]

If the word "origin" here refers to the doctrine, we have only to repeat, what has already been shown, that the origin of the doctrine dates back to the beginning of the Christian Church. As to the rest, we incline to think, that a correct knowledge of the true state of the case would reduce the expression, "almost universally," to "to a considerable extent." If the statement has any particular reference to the Lutheran Church in this country, we can only express that the condition which she was fifty years and more ago is not to be help up in any respect to us as a model. But admitting that at the time and earlier the Lutheran clergy of Germany and many in this country, did forsake, not only as respects the Eucharist, but as regards other doctrines of fundamental importance, the sound Scriptural Confessions of our church, why did they thus abandon her views? Was it not because rationalist speculation and neo-logical exegesis had come into the place of the quiet spirit and the simple faith of the church, and had usurped the authority to decide what the Sacred Word must and must not teach? And if such were according to the doctor's own admission the views of the Lutheran Church up to that time, how can they now be different? Has a general council of the entire Lutheran church altered or abrogated these views? Has the church delegated to him or the general synod, or to anyone else, authority to modify and adapt our doctrines to the speculative ideas of our age?

We say not; we have not yet heard of any formal, universal abrogation of our Confessions; and the event is less likely than ever to occur. Is it not quite noteworthy and thankworthy that, as the pernicious influence and the illusion of modern rationalism and neology in Germany were compelled to give way before the light diffused through the revival of a candid, humble, reverent, and devout study of the

---

[19] Page 34

Scriptures, and as theology again learned submission to the Bible, the most thoroughly educated and enlightened theologians of our Church began to return to the unaltered text of her Confession, the loyal adherents of which are daily increasing in number?

In ' his first section Doctor S. lays down certain "general principles of interpretation" which we have little to say about.[20] The first paragraph contains an assertion concerning the nature of words, which a superficial acquaintance with the subject may seem to warrant, but which, upon thorough research, and a profound study of the sources of our modern languages, is proved to be untenable and utterly incorrect.

As respects his subordination of inspired language to the judgments of natural reason and of common sense, and his rejection, as untrue, of what his natural reason and his common sense cannot approve, though it is the meaning of Scripture literally understood, we had seen this position taken so often before, that it did not at all surprise us to encounter it again here. Hence we took no notice of it at first. We deem it however, proper to state here, that we regard this as essentially and thoroughly rationalistic; and we are satisfied, that whenever this rule or canon comes to be strictly and consistently carried out in its application to revealed truth, by divines of still orthodox churches, we shall soon see that many doctrines, which are now considered fundamental and of paramount importance, among them that of the inseparable union of the divine and human natures in Christ, of the Trinity, and with these, that of redemption, will be cast away. The advocates of the supreme authority of natural reason and common sense, which seem in one person to mean one thing, and to another person some other, cannot consistently adhere to and believe these doctrines.

But in the same place the doctor makes an admission which we might thank him for, if making it had any merit,

---

[20] Page 35

and were not simply ascribed to the fact that its opposite could have asserted only in defiance of what is known to be a general principle, or law of the use of language. We refer to the following statement:

> Yet the great mass of men ordinarily employ words in their natural, most obvious, and literal sense. Therefore, a sound rule of interpretation is that the literal sense must be adhered to in the interpretation of all authors, sacred or profane, until reasons occur to justify us in deviating from it.

We have already shown that in the instance before us, the occasion with all its circumstances requires that we adhere to the literal import of the words. We shall have occasion for further reference to this canon as we are fairly entitled to hold the Doctor strictly to what he so fully recognizes to be true.

We had arrived at this point in our discussion when we read, for the first time, the dissertation on the doctrine of the Eucharist, which Dr. Schmucker appended to the first edition of his translation of Storr and Flatt's Elementary Course of Biblical Theology, published in 1826; Viewed by the side of his article now before us, this dissertation has a peculiar interest. It is composed mainly of extended extracts from the writings of Reinhard and Mosheim, in which it is clearly shown that the words of institution are not, and cannot be, figurative, and the entire consistency of the Lutheran view with Scripture and reason is most effectually vindicated. We do not have room, in this place, to quote from these extracts; we may do so on a subsequent page. If our readers will look them up, and read them in connection with the article to which we are now endeavoring to reply, we promise them that they will find them quite rich and delicious. In his conclusion, the Doctor himself labors very successfully, by a train of reasoning totally different, in the main, from that which we have presented above, to show that the appeal to the "properties and laws of matter," in arguing against the Lutheran view of the Lord's Supper is fallacious and absurd, adding that in view of the church's denial,

> That the glorified body of Christ is possessed of those properties and subject to those laws which we denominate properties and laws of matter, nothing but a want of penetration and logical clearness can induce an honest disputant to charge the doctrine with contradiction.

We agree with this entirely. Again he says:

> As the glorified body of Christ is far more exalted in its properties (i.e. nature) than our material bodies are, it is probable a priori, that these properties may be susceptible to the greatest exaltation from his union with God, without destroying the properties (unknown to us) of his glorified body.

His concluding remark is as follows:

> By these remarks, we wish merely to prove that there is nothing in the nature of this doctrine that can justify us in rejecting it if taught in Scripture, and that as in the case of the doctrine of the Trinity, the only question is: Have the inspired writers taught it? And this question has been fully discussed in the preceding paragraph of our author and in the extracts of Dr. Reinlord.

When we turn our mind from this successful and elaborate attempt to vindicate and put in a positive light the doctrine of our church concerning the Eucharist, to the assault made upon it in the article before us, that our author should have been led through philosophical speculations, to abandon a doctrine which is so obviously taught in sacred Scripture, and of which he should be a prominent defender due to his learning and position.

In proceeding now to examine the article in the last number of the Review, we can of course have only a little to say regarding what is given there as "the literal sense of the words of institution" meaning thereby the Popish interpretation of transubstantiation. We have already denied that this interpretation is literal. We protest emphatically against the manner in which the Savior's words are, in this section, between marks of quotation, amplified, distorted, and made self-contradictory, for the purpose of caricaturing the so-called literal interpretation of the Romanists. Such proceedings are unworthy a grave and dignified divine.[21]

Having disposed of the Romish superstition, Dr. S. proceeds to give what he is pleased to style "the first figurative interpretation (that of Luther)" of the words of the institution, in an imitation, amplification, and a downright caricature of our Savior's language. If the Doctor imagines that such outrages are creditable to himself and those who agree with him, and that they will gain friends to the side which he has espoused, he will, we fancy, find himself sadly mistaken. For our part, we shall not meddle further with his unwarranted and bizarre paraphrase of words, which; in their plain and direct meaning, are susceptible of one widely different from his, as we have already shown; he is welcome to all the praise which his efforts as a caricaturist may procure him. That the Lutheran interpretation is not figurative at all, but the only truly literal one that we know of, we have also fully set forth on a preceding page.

It therefore only remains in this place, that we briefly notice another instance of his promptness to supply words which those, upon whose language he is commenting, never used, and meanings which they never intended. In a note on p. 39, he puts the tenth article of the Augsburg Confession

---

[21] To the writer's strong assertion respecting the superior validity of the testimony of our senses, we have replied in a note on p. 62.

into the following words: "the body and blood of the Lord are truly and substantially (*vere et substantialiter*) present, and tendered and received, as the Romish Church has hitherto believed (*wie man bis anher inder Kirchen gehaltenhat*)." Now this is a downright perversion, an in excusable instance of misrepresentation, and calculated to mislead every reader unacquainted with the German language. The article in question does not say a word about the Romish Church, but speaks of the Church in general terms—of that Church which existed long before Romanism was born; and that the primitive Church held those views, which he is here tirelessly laboring to bring into discredit, we have already proved by the indispensable evidence. But what must honest readers think of a cause which requires such methods of defense as that to which our author has resorted here?

In another note on page 41, he cites the language of the Visitation Articles of Saxony, in order to render that of the Symbolical Books more offensive. We shall only reply here, that it has always been well understood, that the language quoted from the Visitation Articles was never intended to be received in so gross a sense as to identify our Lord's body in the Sacrament with his earthly body, as will, moreover, clearly appear upon a candid examination of the whole context. And, at all events, whatever may be thought of the representation made in these articles, the Symbolical Books of the Lutheran Church are not at all responsible for it: those Articles have never had authority out of Saxony, where sovereign power imposed, and required subscription to them, and hence they ought never to have been printed with the Symbolical Books of our Church, except in an Appendix. We do wish that those who controvert our Confessions would confine themselves to such books as have real symbolical authority.

CHAPTER 6
THE OMNIPRESENCE OF CHRIST

WE proceed. The general drift of the argument advanced by our author under b, c, d, e, on page 41, has already been answered in that part of our discussion, which was written before we received the article before us. We have therefore yet only to attend to a few of his specifications. The manner in which instances are mentioned, in which the risen Savior appeared to one or more of his disciples, and not at the same time to others, amounts to nothing more than transparent special pleading: we might as well be told that when he pronounced the parable of the sower, he was not, at the same time, uttering that of the good Samaritan, and so on. If the risen Savior deemed it proper to show himself on different occasions to one or more of his friends, while others were absent, does this prove anything more than that he chose, in his wisdom, to act so and no otherwise? Does it demonstrate the impossibility of his doing a thousand other things which he did not do? But does our author forget that shortly before his ascension, our Savior ate with (or in the presence of) his disciples? "And they gave him a piece of a broiled fish, and of an honey-comb. And he took it, and did eat before them." Luke 24:42-43. In the narrative found in St. John 21:1-14. The fact that the Savior himself ate on that occasion is not distinctly stated, but it may be justly inferred from all the circumstances of the case.

These events plainly prove that our Lord's human nature was not yet perfectly glorified. And this is equally evident from other considerations, for his body still obviously possessed certain ordinary properties of terrestrial bodies, such as visibility, tangibility, etc. We know very well, that the state which is, in systematic divinity, termed the *status exaltationis*, began with the resurrection; but we conceive it to be indisputable that the Son of Man was not fully glorified, until he ascended to heaven, and sat down at the right hand of the Father Almighty ; and as the controversy respecting the real presence of Christ's body and blood in the Eucharist has reference to his perfectly glorified humanity, the argument here employed by Dr. S. necessarily falls to the ground.

But there is another point, already discussed extensively, to be briefly noticed here: this, namely, that the Lutheran interpretation of the words of institution:

> Contradicts the observation of all ages and nations, that all bodies (material substances) must occupy definite portions of space, and cannot be at more than one place at the same time.[22]

We would merely present a few analogies here from nature, which those who are applying the ordinary laws of matter or corporeity to the glorified body of Christ, may take into serious consideration. The sun is sensibly present throughout at least the whole of our system, by its light, its heat, and its power of attraction, whereby it centralizes the movements of all the bodies that belong to our section of the universe. If a telegraph wire extended, if one unbroken line, from New-York to St. Louis (the effect would be the same if it ran round the globe), and the electric current were passed into it at either terminus, the same electric spark would be at one

---

[22] See the whole statement on p. 41. b.

and the same moment, in St. Louis and New- York, and at all intermediate places, certainly without any appreciable difference of time.[23] More analogies of a similar nature might be given; not, certainly, to prove anything positive respecting the ubiquity of our Lord's glorified humanity, but merely to show, that if material objects with which men are regularly conversant, and which are, in a greater or less degree, subject to the direct inspection of our senses, and even to our control, exhibit such remarkable properties, such astonishing phenomena, it is in the highest degree presumptuous to assert, that the Lord of glory cannot, in his infinitely exalted and glorified humanity, be present, entire and undivided, if it so please him, in all places of his dominions.

On page 42 we find the following assertion: "The alleged 'spiritual' presence of the Savior's body is a contradiction in terms." Is it indeed? Well, we can supply our author with a few more such contradictions, and he may dispose of them as he best can: " It is sown a natural body ; it is raised a spiritual body. There is a natural body, and there is a spiritual body." (1 Cor. 15:44). Really, the apostle Paul shows very little deference to the decisions of philosophers. But here is another:

> But a moral signification, as is evident from the passages just quoted, is far more agreeable to the *usus loquendi* (the current usage of words), and is perfectly easy and natural. The cup of the blessing—is it not the communion, does it not bring us spiritually into communion with the body of Christ,

---

[23] "Electricity passes instantaneously to any distance on the earth's surface." "The news received from foreign countries may reach all parts of the United States at the same moment." "The velocity of electricity amounts to 288,000 miles per second." — Gray's Elements of Natural Philosophy.

etc.[24] What does our friend mean by being brought spiritually into communion with the body of Christ? What does this spiritual communion with a body mean? According to our author it is simply a point-blank contradiction in terms. We, who hold that the reception of the body and blood of Christ in the Eucharist, is, though connected with the reception of material elements, not grossly sensuous, but in an important sense a spiritual communion, have no difficulty with the subject. But more of this when this point comes up in due order.

Having already answered the objections under c, d, and e, we proceed to f., on page 43. It is argued here, that the doctrine of the real presence cannot be true, because the Scriptures represent Christ as having left this world, as having returned to the Father, and as being seated at his right hand in heaven: it is urged, that, "he was carried up into heaven," and that Peter declares, that "the heavens must receive him until the times of the restitution of all things, which God had spoken by the mouth of all his holy prophets, since the world began." etc. If this argument avails anything, it must prove that though there is a divine presence in the Church on earth, the exalted Mediator, the glorified Redeemer, is in heaven, and cannot, therefore, be in his Church, or have anything to do with it, as the God-man. For surely, in his person the two natures are inseparably united, constituting the one only Mediator; and where he is at all, there he is *totus*, entire and undivided.

We are really surprised that a veteran theologian, like Dr. S., should use arguments like this, to prove the impossibility of the glorified Savior's presence, in his personal integrity or entirety, among his people; and especially that he should support his reasoning by an appeal to Matt. 24:23, as if this passage had any connection whatever with the subject in hand, and were not directly intended to caution his disciples

---

[24] Dr. Schmucker on the Nature of the Savior's Presence in the Eucharist: Ev. Rev. for July, 1851, p. 46.

against the pretensions of pseudo-messiahs, and various false rumors. But if this argument has any bearing against the Lutheran view of the Eucharist, its force must reach far beyond this, for it is equally valid as we have seen, against the Savior's being in any sense present in his Church, and indeed, against the entire doctrine of the divine omnipresence. We will not weary our readers by citing the numberless passages in the Old and New Testaments, which, on the one hand, directly declare, and on the other indirectly imply, that God dwells and reigns in heaven : let a single one suffice: "Our Father who art in heaven.'" Now, if the argument under consideration proves, that he, who is in the undivided integrity of his divine and human nature the glorious Head of the Church universal, cannot thus be present among his people on earth, it also proves that the Almighty Father is not and cannot be omnipresent, is not and cannot be present anywhere but in heaven; for this part of the Doctor's argument rests entirely on the declarations that represent Christ as having gone to, and as being in, heaven.

In connection with the passages cited by Dr. S., we may refer here to John 16:16: "A little while, and ye shall not see me: and again, a little while, and ye shall see me, because I go to the Father;" and John 16:22: "And ye now therefore have sorrow; but I will see you again, and your heart shall rejoice, and your joy no man takes from you:"—which seeing of him, after his brief removal, the best commentators understand, for various convincing reasons, to mean the perpetual communion of believers with him.

As respects the passage, Acts 3:21, it is translated, "whom the heaven must receive," and thus quoted here. Does our author not know that, according to the grammatical construction, the words are as readily and correctly translated: "who must take possession of heaven:" ὅν and not οὐρανόν, being the accusative before the infinitive? The use of a middle verb confirms the correctness of this rendering, which is, in every respect, more accordant with the exalted dignity of the personage spoken of, who is constantly represented, not as being carried to heaven by other agents, but as ascending into heaven, and whom St. Paul expressly describes as having "ascended up far above all heavens, that he might Jill all things,'" Eph. 4 10, and not that heaven might so receive him, as there locally to confine and shut him up. And the apostle evidently says this of the glorified Redeemer; for, that God was universally present did not, in this place, demand so solemn an announcement. Of course the whole passage refers to Christ.

In this same connection the author says:

> And although the Savior left on record the delightful promise, that he would be always with his disciples till the end of the world, it was in his divine nature, which is omnipresent; and his next visible appearance, the angels informed the men of Galilee at his ascension, would again be from heaven in like manner as they had seen him ascend.

We should like to ask Dr. S. whether, either in the sanctuary, or at the domestic altar, or in the closet, he ever prays for the divine presence, ever entreats the exalted Mediator and Redeemer to bestow the favor of his gracious presence; and if so, whether he means no more than this, that the divine omnipresence might not be suspended, but be continued unto and over those with and for whom he prays? In fact, this manner of explaining the Savior's delightful promise robs it of all its force, and strips it of all that special comfort, and joy which it was designed to communicate. If it implied no more than the divine omnipresence, then it is simply tantamount to saying: that providence, which, as God, I exercise over all my works, will not be withdrawn from you, but will be over and with you at all times, unto the end of the world. Such promises, rich, indeed, in blessing and comfort, but entirely general, they had doubtless often read in the Old Testament. But the context, the entire occasion, compels the belief that something special and peculiar was intended—that he would be present in his Church and with his people in a peculiar manner, different from his presence in the world by his overruling providence. And we contend, that he promised to be present in the character in which he spoke, as the Son of God and man, in the indivisible oneness of his divine and human nature; nor are we told anywhere, that he is ever otherwise present, in one nature and not in the other. And whether men choose to call this a perpetual miracle or not, the promise remains sure, that the divine and human person constituting the one Mediator will be with his people always, even unto the end of the world.

CHAPTER 7
THE CHARGE OF "CARNAL EATING"

THE next objection raised by Dr. Schmucker appears on page 44:

> Again, whilst the idea, that Christ is figuratively represented as the spiritual food of the believer, is a delightful, consoling and be coming one; the supposition that the believer is to eat the actual flesh of his best friend, and drink his real blood, is a gross, repulsive and unnatural idea, which nothing but the clearest evidence would authorize us to adopt.

"Gross, repulsive, and unnatural idea!" Yes, if we held that gross sort of reception, which Luther calls Capernaitish eating, or if, like the Papists, we taught transubstantiation. But we have spoken of this elsewhere. With reference to the objection here more particularly before us, we, in the first place, translate the following sentences from Sartorius:[25]

---

[25] *Christi Person und Werk.* (Christ's Person and Work)

It is further said, that to partake of Christ's body and blood is a revolting idea: where, however, those who make this objection, themselves carry the revolting element into the idea, by representing to themselves the act, as did the Jews at Capernaum, in the most grossly sensuous and inhuman manner. But there is surely, in another form, a partaking of the flesh and blood of a human being, which, although still very material and sensuous, yet not only presents nothing revolting, but is rather an emblem (Bild) of the tenderest love; we mean this, when a mother nourishes her sucking child with her flesh and blood.[26] But with this also, our partaking of the body and blood of Christ in the Sacrament is not to be compared, because here everything that is materially (or grossly) sensuous is out of the question, and only the supersensuous substance thereof is received with and under the bread and wine. Thus everything offensive and repulsive disappears.

This is well said. But we have yet another, and, we think, most important consideration to urge. If the reception of Christ's body and blood in the Eucharist "is a gross, repulsive, and unnatural idea," what are we to say of the doctrine that mankind were redeemed from sin and eternal death through Christ's atoning sacrifice? It will not, we suppose, be pretended, that Christ came into the world to deliver men from physical infirmities and sufferings, otherwise than indirectly through the cure and removal of that moral disease, by which all sorts of physical sufferings are brought upon the children of men; and certainly the disciples of Christ have not, through their connection with him, obtained exemption from those infirmities and sufferings which are the common

---

[26] We would go still further, and instance the manner in which the life of the unborn child is sustained, nourished, and developed in the mother's womb. Is there anything repulsive or revolting in this? *Verbum sapienti sat.*

lot of humanity. It was the moral, the spiritual relations of mankind to their Creator which he came to restore from the disordered and evil state into which they had fallen to their normal and legitimate condition. He came to save men's souls; to reconcile man as a moral being to his God; to heal his moral diseases; to effect his moral or spiritual renovation; and to fit him for the enjoyment of happiness flowing from moral sources, having a moral or spiritual basis. And yet, notwithstanding this moral or spiritual design of his mission, it was necessary that the Son of God should appear in the flesh; should suffer and bleed and die in the flesh; that his body should be broken and his blood shed, as a propitiatory sacrifice for sin, to which pointed all the sin offerings offered from the beginning of time.

Whatever else was necessary to render the sacrifice effectual, nothing is more certain than that the physical sufferings and death of Christ, as the Lamb of God, were indispensable:

> Forasmuch as ye know that ye were not redeemed with corruptible things, as silver and gold, from your vain conversation received by tradition from your fathers; but with the precious blood of Christ, as of a lamb without blemish and without spot. (1 Pet. 1:18-19)

And while we are told that, "Without the shedding of blood there is no remission," we are also assured that, "The blood of Jesus Christ cleanses from all sin." Now, viewing this subject from the standpoint of the opponents of our Confession, we ask, what means more gross and unnatural could have been employed to effect the great moral ends of the gospel scheme? What idea can be more repulsive than this, that, in order to accomplish the reconciliation of man's soul with the Eternal Spirit, such a bodily sacrifice, such physical sufferings and death of the innocent Jesus should have been imperatively necessary? God forbid that we should intimate, that in all this there is aught gross, repulsive and unnatural; but we do say, that, if this charge lies against the Lutheran view, not misstated or distorted, respecting the Eucharist, it holds with equal comprehensiveness and force against the doctrine of atonement through a bleeding and crucified Savior. We see nothing gross, repulsive, or unnatural in either doctrine, but those who make such objections against the one, are bound, in consistency, to make them against the other.

As respects the remarks at the close of this section, 9., with respect to the term spiritual applied by the Form of Concord to eating and drinking material flesh and blood, (remember that Lutherans believe that Christ's body is glorified), in a manner utterly unintelligible, we do not consider it necessary to say more, than that to us it is quite as intelligible as Dr. Schmucker's assertion, that the cup of blessing brings us spiritually into communion (i.e. spiritual communion) with the body of Christ.[27]

---

[27] See page 46

CHAPTER 8
THE EUCHARIST IN 1 CORINTHIANS

NEXT, our author proceeds to examine "several expressions in the portion of Scripture discussing this subject, which have been supposed to favor Luther's interpretation." He works hard to show that they can have no such meaning. The first passage which passes through the ordeal of his criticism is 1 Cor. 11:27.[28] Hear our author:

> It has been said, "How could we be guilty of the body of Christ, if it were not present?" We answer; To be guilty of the body, means in the original, to be guilty or commit sin in reference to the body; that is, to make the body of Christ the occasion of committing sin.

Very well said. But how this is to be accomplished, except that body be present, is far beyond our feeble powers of comprehension. To treat with irreverence, or to insult, on earth, a body that is in heaven, and far above all heavens, is a mystery entirely too deep for us to penetrate. However, we are having help. The Doctor proceeds, and gives us as

---

[28] The reader is referred to p. 45 of the July No. of the Review.

wonderful a piece of argumentation as we have ever had the pleasure of examining:

> And must not all admit that we can and often do commit sin in regard to absent persons or things? May we not sin, or be guilty, in regard to an absent friend (rather a shabby sort of friendship this, at all events), by slandering or even thinking ill of him, just as well as when he is present?

Why yes, to be sure; but what in all the world can this have to do with our friend's body, unless we go and commit assault and battery upon him? And even if, when he is absent, we were to say of him, that he is a model of ugliness, and this were to be repeated to him, we think that he would regard the offence as committed, not against his body, but against him, the intellectual and moral man, our friend. We go on. "Do we not insult the majesty of an absent king, when we treat with indignity a monument or other memorial which has been established in honor of him?" Yes, surely we grant, that, if he were to hear of such disrespectful proceedings, his pride might be offended, his dignity wounded, his conscious soul aggrieved; but unless, in addition to all this, we should assail him personally and lay violent hands on him, his body would, we conceive, care nothing at all about the affair, and certainly be none the worse for it. No sir, no!

We must keep serious. And we do most solemnly contend, that this very declaration of St. Paul is one which the opponents of the Lutheran Confession never can get over, never can torture to say anything else, than that unworthy communicants are guilty of the body and blood of the Lord; guilty of insulting and treating with irreverence and indignity the body and blood of our Lord, because his body and blood are present in the Holy Sacrament, which such unworthy communicants dishonor, by not discerning, not bearing in mind and devoutly considering, that it is the glorified body of Christ which, in mysterious connection with the visible elements, is presented to them; by not receiving it with a believing and loving soul, and therefore by treating it with irreverence and disrespectfully. If the apostle had meant only that the unworthy communicant treated his absent Savior with disrespect and indignity, why did he not say so? Why did he not say "guilty of sinning against Christ" or "guilty of sinning against Jesus?" But not meaning this, he says what he does mean: "guilty of sinning against the body and blood of the Lord" thereby distinctly declaring, that he regards the Savior as, in his glorified humanity, actually present in the Eucharist; so that he who partakes unworthily of the bread and wine, treats with disrespect and irreverence what is most sacred, and thus incurs unspeakable guilt.

As respects the passage quoted from St. James, it has not the slightest connection with the matter in hand. It is not the word "guilty," but the words "guilty of the body and blood," which are under discussion; and moreover, the man who knowingly and willfully breaks one divine command, thereby shows that he has no respect for God's law; that he is ready for any sin; and thereby actually, virtually offends against the whole law. We cannot in any way discover, by what principle of exegesis this passage is brought to bear unfavorably upon the subject under discussion. The same remark applies to what follows on this 45th page. This is precisely the guilt of unworthy communicants, that they do not distinguish between the eating and drinking in the Eucharist, and their ordinary eating and drinking; that they do not consider what a sacred object is offered to them in the celebration of that solemn rite. Men may explain as much as they please, to the end of time, and they will never get rid of the overwhelming power of 1 Cor. 11:27.

The second passage examined by our author, is 1 Cor. 10:16.[29] He gives a number of different significations in which the word κοινωνία (communion, fellowship), is used, and cites passages to establish and illustrate his definitions. Now it may

---

[29] See p. 46.

be quite interesting to show that κοινωνία has different meanings; but what has all this philological criticism to do with the matter in hand? The particular signification of a word that has many meanings, must be determined by the particular context in which it occurs, just as in English we determine from the connection, whether the word press means a crowd of people, or a wardrobe, or a machine for printing, or a cheese-press. The whole argument here is as irrelevant and inconsistent, as cloudy and confused, as the one on p. 45, about ενόκος.

None of the Doctor's citations make anything against the Lutheran doctrine concerning the Eucharist, and some of them fully confirm the correctness of our view. Thus, for example, he refers to Rom. 15:26 and 2 Cor. 9:13 as passages in which κοινωνία signifies "communication or bestowment of a benefit, beneficence." Now we do not at all object to thus translating the word in these passages; but how came it here to have this signification? In two ways. Firstly, because the bestowment of a benefit establishes a peculiar communion or fellowship between the donors and receivers; but secondly, and chiefly, because in the one case the Macedonians and Achaians made up their "benefit" by a joint collection, by uniting and fellowshipping in raising a contribution. In the other text, the same is reported of the Corinthians. It is not the benefit, but the manner of it, that gave rise to this use of the word. We have neither time nor space to bestow upon his other meanings, and the passages cited to confirm them; nor is it necessary, as they cannot alter, or in any way affect, the significations of the word in the passage under consideration.

The point to be determined here is, what is meant by the communion of the body and blood of our Lord; and that it can mean anything else than direct, actual communion, it is impossible to prove, and idle to assert. Dr. S., evidently conscious of the difficulty under which he labors here, comes to the conclusion already referred to: "The cup of blessing — is it not the communion, does it not bring us spiritually into communion with the body of Christ,"—in which, altering the apostle's language, he makes the cup the communion of the body. But as he has decided[30] that anything spiritual affirmed concerning bodies, or anything spiritually affirmed respecting them, is a contradiction in terms, we do not see why we should give ourselves any further trouble on this point.

But he goes on to speak of 1 Cor. 10:18: "Are not they who eat of the sacrifices, partakers of the altar?" We cannot discover what service this passage is to render him here. Communion with the altar and participation in the blessing connected with its sacred use, were in part effected by eating the sacrifice which lay upon the altar. The presence of Christ's body and blood, in connection with visible signs, renders the Eucharist a Sacrament, a sacred mystery. We partake of the fullness of its blessing, by receiving, in, with, or under the consecrated elements, the body and blood of that Lamb that was slain for the remission of sins. While we admit that, 1 Cor. 10:16., does not definitely determine anything as respects the relation of Christ's body and blood, in the Sacrament, to the bread and wine, but only asserts positively our communion with his body and blood, verse 18 can, by no ingenuity, be made to say anything against our view. It is, as far as it has any bearing upon the subject before us, decidedly in our favor. All the sacrifices under the old covenant were types of Christ, our sin-offering, and in the fact, that a great part of the victim was eaten, we can scarcely help discovering some typical reference to the mysteries of the Sacrament of the altar. As to what the Doctor says about the Jews eating the God whom they worshipped, we have nothing to do with, or to say about, such enormities.

Our author next cites verse 20 and then asks: "Who would suppose that the gentiles, in their sacrifices, had communion with the bodies of the dead heroes and demigods whom they worshipped?" No one, probably, entertains any such nonsense. "Yet, if the word κοινωνία in the one case

---

[30] Page 42

means the actual participation of the flesh and body of the being commemorated, what reason can be as signed for its having so different a signification in the other?" Why simply this, that in the one case the body and blood are distinctly specified, in the other not; and that communion with a body can only mean what the words directly express, while fellowship with devils may be entirely spiritual, or, for aught we know to the contrary, bodily. And yet there is even here a singular circumstance to be noted, viz. that the gods were supposed to feast upon, or to eat the sacrifices offered them; so that even here there is an eating in the case, which fact we do not mention because we attach any importance to the crude notions of the heathens, but because it is quite remarkable that the κοινωνία was supposed to be effected by means of eating, in which the Gentiles considered both parties to take part.

CHAPTER 9
THE COMMUNICATION OF ATTRIBUTES

WE have now reached that part of our author's treatise, in which he contests the doctrine of the hypostatic union of the two natures in Christ's person, and of the consequent *communicatio idiomatum*, which has been so fully developed, and so clearly and satisfactorily set forth, by later Lutheran divines, in strict accordance with Luther's view, as derived from, and based upon, the Sacred Scriptures. Here then is the proper place to present an extended discussion of this doctrine, which is of essential importance, not only to our doctrine concerning the Eucharist, but equally so to that of the atonement. But ere we proceed to perform this duty, we shall first dispose of a few detached positions taken in the dissertation before us: to take up in detail, and answer extensively, all the assertions made, all the positions taken, all the criticisms presented, all the conclusions drawn, in the whole course of the Doctor's argument, would lead us entirely too far. We shall, therefore, merely place a general disquisition in opposition to his general train of reasoning.

But, for the present, we are to instance a few prominent particulars. And first, he again asserts that Luther himself in part rejected a theological argument or theory in favor of the presence of the body of the Savior in the Lord's Supper, more amply developed since his time. He again fails to specify the particular view which Luther is alleged to have rejected, and we, left to conjecture, and supposing that he alludes to the affair referred to near the commencement of our present article, simply assert in reply, that the Doctor is misinformed. We know of no doctrinal point respecting the Lord's Supper which Luther, when once he had taken this ground, ever gave up.

Secondly, Colossians 2:9: "For in him dwells all the fullness of the Godhead bodily." Dr. S. explains this passage as follows:

> This passage we think naturally signifies. In Christ the real not imaginary, the full divinity and not an inferior deity dwells; that is, with his human nature the truly divine nature is really not figuratively, or typically, but actually united σωματικῶς personally, that is, into one person.

This exposition is simply our author's own, entirely arbitrary, and fortified by not one satisfactory reason. In the first place, how can St. Paul be suspected of having even for one moment thought of inferior deities in this connection? Does he ever manifest any fear, lest those whom he addressed should conceive that some fabulous divinity of heathen mythology had become united to the person of Christ? We do not understand how inferior deities can at all come into consideration here. But again, we fear that Dr. S. has but a very indifferent opinion of St. Paul's philological acquirements, and power of language. If the apostle meant to say: really, truly, actually, verily, fully, why did he not use one of the many words which his know ledge of the copious Greek language afforded him, to express this meaning? Why, if he meant no more than this, did he make a new word to express a distinct and different meaning?

For, be it observed, neither the adjective σωματικός nor the adverb σωματικῶς is a classical word. Both occur only in ecclesiastical writers, by whom they were doubtless adopted from the New Testament, in which the adverb under consideration occurs only in this one place. According to the Doctor's criticism, both of this passage and of 1 Cor. 11:27, St. Paul must be regarded (and what right have we thus to criticize an inspired writer) as having indulged in an extraordinary infelicity of expression, if by ςωμα and αιμα he did not mean body and blood, and by σωματικῶς not bodily, but really, truly, fully. The other passages of Scripture here cited have no bearing on the case, for they are not parallel; and the quotations from the classics have no more to do with the matter than the death-song of Regner Lodbrok. If they determine anything at all with regard to the matter before us, it must be by serving to show that the apostle's language means that the person of the Godhead dwells in Christ; which, we acknowledge, would be quite unintelligible to us. St. Paul cannot here have intended to inform the Colossians merely, that the Deity was united with humanity in Christ's person; this idea he could have expressed and did elsewhere express, in suitable language: he evidently meant what he does say, viz. that the fullness of the divine nature pervaded Christ's body, and that thus his humanity was made to partake fully of the Divine nature. We commend to consideration the following exposition of this pas sage by Dr. Albert Barnes, whose critical vision was not blinded by polemic zeal against the doctrine of the *communicatio idiomatum*: and although his explanation does not satisfy us entirely, it goes far be yond Dr. Schmucker's interpretations. We cite only the interpretation: "The fair sense of the phrase is, that the fullness of the divine nature became incarnate, and was indwelling in the body of the Redeemer." Again:

> The meaning is, that it was not any one attribute of the Deity that became incarnate in the Savior; that he was not merely endowed with the knowledge, or the

power, or the wisdom of God, but that the whole Deity thus became incarnate, and appeared in human form.

Thirdly, Matt. 23:18. It is astonishing how the necessity of gathering up arguments, so as to bolster up a theory, can lead men to misunderstand the language of Scripture. A number of passages are here cited to show that ἐχουσία, power, means, in this place, "Not power or omnipotence; but all or full authority to command and direct all things on earth to the accomplishment of the purposes of his mediatorial reign." Is this really all that is expressed by the words: "All power [or, if you will, authority] in heaven and on earth?" If so, we shall have to go to school again, to learn the use and power of words. Admitting even, that the Savior told his disciples this for the purpose of assuring them, that he was able to control and over rule all things for the good of his church, he grounds his declaration upon the fact that all power, all authority, in heaven and on earth, was vested in him. And suppose even this were no appeal to his omnipotence, what matters that, if, according to other Scripture passages, e.g. Phil. 3:21, he possesses this attribute? Hence even the angels worship him: "Jesus Christ, who is gone into heaven, and is on the right hand of God, angels, and authorities, and powers being made subject to him" (1 Pet. 3:22).

To the doctrine of the ubiquity of the body of Christ, our author brings forth numerous, and as he thinks, formidable objections:

1. "The idea that the properties of one substance can become the properties of a different substance is a philosophical absurdity."

Is it indeed? Why there are hundreds of chemical processes which directly contradict this statement; but we cannot stay to specify. We shall, however, present a few facts, by which this philosophical absurdity is effectually done away with. Canton's Phosphorus, and a variety of other substances, upon being exposed to the light, themselves become luminous, so as to give out light in the dark; and this property they retain for some time. Again, when you isolate a man by placing him upon glass, and then, having brought him into communication with a foreign and different object, in the shape of an electric machine, and pass into him a stream of the electric fluid, you may perfectly saturate him with electricity, making this so completely, for a time, a property of his whole body, that, touch him at any point, you draw forth electric sparks; and yet, though electricity has thus temporarily become a property of his body, its own properties remain the same, undergoing no change.

The next is better. When hardened steel is brought into contact with a magnet, it becomes magnetic; in other words, the properties of the magnet become the properties of the steel, which retains them permanently, and in effective activity, without therefore losing any of its own properties, and without robbing the magnet of its properties. But we have a still stronger case. At the marriage in Cana our Lord commanded the servants to fill six large water pots with water. They did so, and they all knew that nothing but water had been put into the pots; and when now he ordered them to draw out, and to bear unto the governor of the feast, it was found to be wine, much better than they had yet had: the distinctive properties of the water had dis appeared, and it had received in their place, to all intents and purposes, as evidenced by the senses of sight and taste, the properties of excellent wine. The case affords a perfect refutation of our author's assertion. Of course, the plea that this was a miracle, can be of no possible use to him, because we are speaking now of that very person who produced this miracle; and the only question at issue here is, whether it is possible for the properties of one object or substance to become the properties of another object or substance, which is here conclusively demonstrated by a plain matter of fact.

2. "It is impossible, in the nature of things, that the infinite properties of God, the uncreated one, should be communicated to any creature." This assertion, if it were true,

would be utterly subversive of the doctrine of Christ's Divinity. If the declaration of Scripture that God became incarnate, means nothing more than that God employed a human being, called Jesus of Nazareth, as an instrument for the manifestation of his goodness, compassion and love towards our race, without communicating to that personage his own divine attributes, then, certainly, Trinitarians are making a very needless ado about the divinity of Christ; for this is precisely what we assert, in opposition to Unitarians and Socinians, not only that there are three persons in the Deity but that Christ Jesus, the Mediator, is, in his entire personality, Divine, and the Second Person in the Trinity. If the human nature and form of Christ were nothing but a mask, behind and under which the Almighty spoke and acted, leaving that nature entirely unaffected by the indwelling Divinity, entering into no absolute, intimate, inseparable union with it, communicating to it no divine attributes, the whole event ceases to be anything more wonderful than the inspiration of the prophets, and we can only be surprised that St. Paul should speak of it as a great mystery:

> Without controversy, great is the mystery of godliness: God was manifest in the flesh, justified in the spirit, seen of angels, preached unto the Gentiles, believed on in the world, received up into glory. (1 Tim. 3:16)

But such positions are wide of the truth. To use Dr. Schmucker's own language, only beginning with as for if, and referring to the expositions of the *Communio naturarum*, and of the *Communicatio idiomatum*, for a full exhibition of our meaning, we say: "as the human nature of Christ acquired possession of divine attributes, it must itself be divine." "Yes, the finite has become infinite, the creature has become the Creator, and a feeble mortal like unto us, in all things, sin only excepted, has become the immortal God." To deny this, as herein after explained, is Docetism and Socinianism. We by no means intend to charge our author with these heresies. We know that he hates them as much as we do; but we contend that he makes assertions in this article, which, when carried out into their logical consequences, must lead to them.

Nor is the Doctor happier in stating:

3. This general principle, that "wherever any one divine attribute is found, there the others must also be, and that is God." This is not as universally and absolutely true as is here taken for granted. Is foreknowledge, the power of foreseeing, and distinctly foretelling very remote future events, a divine attribute? Yes. But prophets and apostles possessed it, without having all, and becoming gods. Is the power of working miracles, of controlling nature, of healing diseases with a word or a touch, nay, of raising the dead, a divine attribute? Yes, yet prophets and apostles possessed and exercised it, thus showing that God can delegate, in a measure, to ordinary human beings, attributes entirely his own, without making them his equals. How different, however, is the case of our Lord Jesus Christ, in whom dwells all the fullness of the godhead bodily, and who himself bestowed upon his servants a mea sure of those powers which we have just instanced.

4. "If the hypostatic union in Christ implies a communication of attributes, it must be reciprocal, and whilst the humanity of Christ is clothed in the attributes of divinity, his divinity must also have assumed the attributes of humanity; have become human; which the opponents are unwilling to admit."

This is a mere assumption, an authoritative dictum, which we reject. We do admit, and most firmly believe that the Scriptures speak truth when they say, that "the Word was made flesh", that "God was manifest in the flesh," i.e. accepted, received, assumed, took to himself our nature, in all its essential attributes ; from which sin is, of course, excluded. Dr. Schmucker himself says in his usual guarded phraseology:

> Yet with the man Jesus there was united another invisible being, of a very different nature and higher order, called Son of God, and united in such a manner as to form a just basis for the reciprocal ascription of attributes taken from either nature, to the one being or person.[31]

United means made one with. If Christ is one being or person, it is perfectly obvious that the two natures in him cannot merely be loosely associated with each other, but must be united in the most intimate and inseparable union. It is impossible to conceive, that there could be a real, veritable unity or oneness of person in Christ, unless there were an actual inter communication of natures, if neither nature communicated anything to the other. If there be no intercommunication of natures, hence no communion of natures, how can it be said that "the Word was made flesh" —in other words, that God became man? Then can the union be fitly likened only to a double wax figure, consisting of two figures glued together at the side or back; and the acts of this double person would be like the interlocking of two cog-wheels. And, if the union is like this, how can it communicate an infinite value to the obedience, the sufferings and death of the man Jesus, if the divine Logos merely exists alongside of him, without partaking of his sufferings, in consequence of the assumption of human nature, of its essential properties? If, on the one hand, the divine nature does not participate in the states and sufferings of the human, and, on the other hand, the human nature does not, beyond and over its natural finite, limited properties, receive also the essential *idiomata* of the divine, the unity or oneness of person which we are taught to believe exists in Christ, must be regarded as impossible. The Scriptures positively declare, that "the Logos became flesh," that he "was made in the likeness of men," and what else can this

---

[31] Pop. Theol. p. 55.

mean, than that he assumed the attributes, the essential properties of humanity? And, although we may truly say, that humanity has nothing to confer or bestow upon God, not having anything that it has not received from God, it is evident, being clearly and fully revealed in Scripture, that it pleased the second hypostasis in the Deity to take upon him all the properties of humanity, without its sin, not of course, thereby to enrich and ennoble himself, but to enrich, elevate and ennoble human nature, and to assimilate it to the divine.[32]

5. "If this hypostatic union," says our author, "is attended by a transfer of attributes, it necessarily involves a confusion of natures, which error was condemned by the ancient church in the Eutychians. And if it was such as to preserve the attributes of each nature distinct, then there can be no real transfer of attributes."

Answer: We teach that in Christ there were two natures in one person. Does Dr. S. deny, that in Christ the divine and human natures are intimately and inseparably united, so as to constitute the one God-man? If not, (and without running into positive heresy, he cannot), he has, if he refuses to adopt the distinct definitions of the Lutheran Church, no alternative but to mix up the two natures in indiscriminate confusion; for there is no way of keeping them distinct, while yet inseparably united, except by receiving the doctrine of the *communicatio idiomatum*, without utterly denying the validity and efficacy of the atonement.[33]

6. "The doctrine," we are further told, "of the ubiquity of Christ's body, instead of conferring more

---

[32] On the reciprocal communication of attributes or properties, see Thomasius: "*Beitrsege zur kirchlichen Christologie*," a translation of which is in course of publication in the Evangelical Review. The reader is also referred to: *Das Bekenntniss der Ev. Luth. Kirche* in *der Consequenz seines Princips*, von Thomasius, p. 204.

[33] For a more extended discussion of this point, as also of the Doctor's 9th objection, we refer to the remarks on the *Comm. Idiomatum* on a following page.

importance on the Eucharist, actually robs it of all special interest, and gives no more to the Sacrament than to every other object and place. We may upon this theory, as well say that Christ's body is in, with or under, every apple and pear, peach and cake, as in the consecrated bread."

This is a strange position for a believer in the Bible to take. Granted, that we hold that, by virtue of the hypostatic union and the consequent *communicatio idiomatum*, Christ is omnipresent in both his natures, or rather in the undivided integrity of his person, does this prove that he is not present in the Eucharist in a peculiar manner, for a special purpose, to be received in a special, mysterious and inexplicable manner by those who engage in this ordinance? Does the certainty of God's omnipresence prove, that all that we read in the Old Testament respecting his being, in a special manner, for the communication of special favors, and the accomplishment of special purposes, with Moses, with Israel in the desert, in the tabernacle, in the temple, with Samuel and other judges, with David and other godly kings, with prophets, with armies, and with many pious individuals, is all false, simply because some men assert, that there can be no special presence where there is a general omnipresence? Nothing but the great length of this article prevents us from inserting here, Luther's admirable reasoning on this point.[34]

7. "Nay, this doctrine is not entirely exempt from liability to the charge of favoring pantheism."

With what characteristic circumspection this statement is worded. The subject embraced by this paragraph is one of vast compass and profound mystery,[35] and to discuss it here at length would lead us entirely too far. And therefore we simply reply to this objection, that our doctrine is not one iota more liable to the charge of favoring pantheism, than is the doctrine of the divine omnipresence, and that Dr. S. knows very well.

---

[34] See the work above referred to, p. 158. Note.
[35] See Knapp's Theology, Vol. I. p. 202

8. "If," says our author further, "the glorified body of Christ is really in, with, or under the bread, it will be very proper to direct our worship towards the bread, and thus adore the present God-man who is somehow connected with it."

This objection is so puerile and scandalous, that it does not deserve a reply. Dr. S., however, answers it himself in the concluding lines of this paragraph. He seems to see quite satisfactory reason for doing what he is pleased here sneeringly to censure. "For," says he,

> We know that his divine nature is there, as it is omnipresent: and therefore we would have as much reason to worship towards the bread as if he were personally and visibly to appear in connection with it.

If, then, the presence of Christ's divine nature, which he allows, constitutes, as he here asserts, as much reason to worship towards the bread as if he were personally and visibly to appear in connection with it, we do not see on what grounds he abstains from an act, the propriety of which he thus alleges. It is quite obvious that he perceives a reason for the act, quite independent of the sacramental presence which we advocate. We are well satisfied to receive the consecrated elements in the Eucharist, in the manner prescribed by our Lord himself; to our author we leave the satisfaction of engaging in the Popish worship of the consecrated bread, as he seems to be thoroughly convinced of its propriety.

CHAPTER 10
THE EUCHAIRST IN JOHN 6

Finally, our author totally denies that our Lord's discourse, recorded John 6:25-56 has any reference to the Holy Supper. We shall presently show that it has, but we must first notice briefly two particular objections advanced in this connection.

1."If this passage (John 6:56) teaches a physical eating and indwelling of the Savior's body in the communicant, it also affirms that the communicant's body dwells in the body of the Savior, which is absurd."

True enough, absurd. Our author reasons here again on the assumption, that Lutherans teach a gross, materially sensuous, Capernaitish eating of Christ's body; but while we believe that the Savior's glorified humanity is, in a mysterious, inexplicable manner, received by the communicant in partaking of the bread and wine, and see no difficulty in the case at all, we know very well that our gross, material and polluted bodies cannot be transferred into his glorified body; we do not believe that the Scriptures teach impossibilities. We admit that this, our dwelling in Christ, is by faith, and Dr. S. ought to know that his inference here is a non sequitur, just as much so, as if he were to maintain that, because Jehovah dwelt, in the visible form of the Shekinah, in the tabernacle and in the temple of the Old Covenant, therefore the tabernacle and the temple dwelt bodily in him, and that the Jewish nation had dwelt bodily in God, because Moses addressed the Lord thus: "Lord, thou hast been our dwelling-place in all generations." Our dwelling in Christ is represented here as the effect or result of our receiving him, and is further explained in the following verse: "he that eats me, even he shall live by me," and thus we are really in him, in a spiritual sense, in that he is our life; that in him we live, and move, and have our being physically, and that out of him we have no spiritual life at all.

2. A few words on the assertion, that "the union of the two natures in Christ" "produced not even a shadow of a *communicatio idiomatum* (transfer or communication of attributes) on earth," here follow inferences. How can our author hazard such an assertion, in the face of such passages as Matt. 28:18, John 5:22, 26-27? That omnipotence belonged to God; that the right to judge all men, and the authority to execute judgment, pertains to God, the disciples knew, and had no need of being so solemnly informed, even if to communicate this information had been (which is quite out of the question) the Savior's design. There is nothing more perfectly clear than this, that the Savior here declares, in his human nature, that omnipotence and the authority to hold the judgment, were conferred upon him. It was not necessary to give his divine nature what this already possessed: no, he himself adds in verse 27: "because he is the Son of Man."

We are now ready for the general question, whether John 6:25-56 has any reference to the Lord's Supper.[36] That such was the view held by the primitive Church, is certain; so that "even Lampe," who would have been glad to deny it, if this had been possible, "is compelled to acknowledge: It cannot be denied that the majority of the Fathers understood

---

[36] The substance of our remarks on this point, and the sentences in marks of quotation, are taken from Stier's Commentary, Vol. IV. p. 310.

this portion of Scripture to speak of a sacramental manducation."[37]

> Nothing is more simple than the view which was held of old, that the Evangelist John, who records historically neither the appointment of baptism, nor the institution of the Lord's Supper, reports instead, how, in Chap, 6, the Lord speaks prophetically of the essential nature of baptism, and here, in Ch. 6, in like manner of the Holy Supper. Thus much, at least, von Gerlach also admits: "as baptism is the sacrament of regeneration through water and the Spirit, so is the Holy Supper of our Lord the Sacrament of this restoration to life, and renewal through the flesh and blood of Christ, and sustains therefore the same relation to this discourse, as baptism to the conversation with Nicodemus."

There is an obvious reciprocal relation between the discourse in this chapter, and the words of the institution, which renders it proper, and even necessary, to explain each by the other, just as the works of God throw the right light upon his words, and vice versa, his words throw the right light upon his works. The connection is so obvious here, that it is impossible to conceive how Luther and other critics should have failed to perceive and urge it.

> Can it be conceived that our Lord, when, being on the point of giving his flesh for the life of the world, he ordained for the future the eating of his body and the drinking of his blood, should not have had in his mind what he had said in Capernaum, and not have reminded his disciples of it? That the two should be without any connection? It will always be impossible

---

[37] "Negari nequit, Patrum maximum numerum nostrum locum de sacramentali manducatione in tellexisse."

for us to assert any such thing. And if, as would be natural, it should at the same time be said, that Christ, when discoursing at Capernaum, had not at all thought of the future Sacrament, we regard this as equally impossible, and inconceivable. Bengel says: "This Sacrament is of such importance, that it may be readily conceived, that Jesus, just as he predicted the treachery of Judas (v. 71), and his death, had in the same manner predicted, a year before (its institution), also the Sacred Supper, of which he was certainly thinking while uttering these words, in order that his disciples might afterwards remember his prediction. This whole discourse respecting the flesh and blood of Jesus Christ, has reference to his passion, and with it to the Sacred Supper. For this reason the flesh and blood are throughout mentioned separately."[38]

Admitting that there may be an extra-sacramental communion, a spiritual reception of his flesh and blood by faith:

> This cannot be regarded as a *spiritualis fruitio* or *manducatio* in the strictest sense, as opposed to all corporeity; for without, as well as in, the Sacrament, that which we received remains truly flesh and blood, and consequently there is an eating and drinking with the mouth of the inward man. And hence the words of the institution are to be interpreted according to John 6, and, in return, the very words of the institution serve to show, that the Savior here had the Sacred Supper in his mind, and that he intended, by this discourse, to prepare the minds of his disciples

---

[38] Tanti hoc sacramentum est momenti, ut facile existimari possit, Jesum, ut proditionem Judæ? v. 71., et mortem suam, ita etiam S. Coenam, de qua inter haec verba certissime secum cogitavit, uno ante anno praedixisse, ut discipuli possent prae- dictionis postea recordari. Tota haec de carne et sanguine J. C. oratio passionem spectat et cum ea S. Ccenam. Hinc separata carnis et sanguinis mentio constanter.

for the institution of that solemn rite. And precisely because they were Jews, they could understand the real eating and drinking of flesh and blood, offered in sacrifice, much better than the ideal reception of our speculative theologians, had they not been blinded by the prejudice, which led them to take offence at the human personality in which he appeared . . . especially as, about this time, the reference to the paschal lamb was obvious to the hearers, as well as to the speaker.

Even the incorrigibly perverse Lange maintains here that τρωγειν; used for θαγειν, can only mean to eat, really and veritably." It is here, however, in respect of this discourse in the 6th chapter of John's gospel, that the figurative theory is most strenuously insisted upon, and most liberally applied. Dr. S. even refers us to verse 63 to prove by it the justness of his figurative interpretation, thus only showing, that he has failed to discover the correct interpretation of this verse. The whole context shows, that it was designed to set right the Jews, who so perversely and grossly misunderstood him, as though he had meant that they should eat him bodily as he there stood before them, and as an ordinary human being, such as they conceived him to be. Our Lord graciously condescends to correct their error, and his words are obviously to be thus interpreted : what you understand me to mean, is not what I intend: mere flesh, flesh per se, as flesh destitute of spirit, which you think I am speaking of, that indeed can profit nothing, cannot make alive.

But how comes it to be overlooked that in this verse the Savior does not, as elsewhere in this chapter, say: "my flesh?" Will any one affirm respecting his flesh, his body, that it profits nothing? And if the Lord had said this of his own flesh, would he not have contradicted what he had, a few minutes before, said, when he told them directly, in verse 51, that his flesh was the life of the world? But when Dr. S. explains this: "Here the Savior seems expressly to teach, that the literal eating of his flesh would profit them nothing," how is it that he does not perceive that, if his explanation were correct, this verse would just as clearly and positively teach, that the literal crucifixion of his flesh, the literal breaking of his body on the cross, would profit them nothing? If he insists upon his interpretation, on the grounds alleged, in the one case, he must, to be consistent, accept it in the other. Here then we say with Stier:

> As regards these words of the Lord, we protest, again and again, against all talk about 'figurative forms of speech.' We consider it entirely unworthy of the Lord, that 'all these forcibly impressive, repeated, accumulated figures should denote nothing more than the spiritual connection with him,'

As says J. von Muller. In conclusion on this point, we translate Stier's concluding remarks on verse55. After insisting that αληθως and not as Lachmann prefers, αληθης is the correct reading, he proceeds:

> Away then, in the presence of this αληθως, with all idealities, put in the place of βρωσις, ποσις, φαγειν and πινειν, and even in the place of ςαρχ, and with all abstractions designed to explain the truth which is given in the words of Jesus, whilst, in reality, they detract from and enfeeble it. The Savior certainly did not ordinarily speak in a manner so grossly corporeal, but had, on the contrary, at all times spiritual words for spiritual things, and when he spoke figuratively, he never did it in such a way that the figure was greater than the thing signified: with him figure was reality, as his own name is reality.[39] If it was here his design to be understood only in a spiritual sense, why did he not employ the expressions so frequently used elsewhere, which are surely plain and strong enough,

---

[39] Bild ist bei ihm Wesen, so wie ein Name Wesen ist.

and why did he not retain as sufficient the more spiritual term: Bread of Life? Why does he speak also of flesh, and even of blood? In the word 'bread' there was figure enough to make his meaning clear: but the words 'flesh and blood,' taken merely as a figure, could contribute nothing to the elucidation of his meaning. And when he moreover perceived, how greatly the Jews, and even many of his disciples, were offended at his words, how imperatively did his wisdom as a teacher, and his love, require that he should clear up the misconception, in such words, perhaps, as these: as ye eat meat (flesh) and bread, and thereby receive it into yourselves, so shall ye receive me into your hearts. But, in the very face of the doubts of the Jews, he goes on to express what he had said, in still stronger language, and leaves them no other conclusion, than that they must eat his flesh and drink his blood. Nay he says expressly (emphatically) my flesh is (truly) meat indeed, and my blood is (truly) drink indeed, (truly, used in each instance); and this is the reverse of figurative and unreal.[40] Yes truly, as even Lange premises, without knowing what a sentence he thus pronounces upon his own subsequent abstractions: He declared in a manner so concrete, so definite, the truth that with his flesh and blood he was the real life-bread of the world.

---

[40] Kapff, Communionbuch, p. 74.

CHAPTER 11
LUTHERAN CHRISTOLOGY

WE proceed now to present, in as brief a space as possible, the view which, according to our Confessions, our Church still holds and defends, respecting the union of the two natures in Christ, and the *communicatio idiomatum*, the communication of divine attributes to Jesus the Son of Man. In no Church has a profound, thoroughly scriptural, and perfectly consistent Christology been so fully developed, and so satisfactorily stated, strictly on the basis of revealed truth, as in ours. Several distinguished living divines of Germany have produced most admirable works on the great theme, and among these none has written with more clearness, and more triumphantly confuted the objections of opponents, than Thomasius, in his *"Beitrage zur Kirchlichen Christologie."* In order to exhibit this subject in all its fullness, it would be necessary to translate this entire work, but the dimensions, to which this article has already grown, barely leave us room for two fragmentary extracts, in which a great deal that precedes them is assumed to be now perfectly understood. He concludes his work, by presenting, under five distinct heads, the great truths which, in the preceding dissertations, he had completely vindicated against the objections of all sorts of opponents; the first exhibits in full the Scripture doctrine of the hypostatic union; the second that of the *communio naturarum*; the third that of the *communicatio idiomatum*. We can barely make room for the second and third, marking them I and II.

I. The *Communio Naturarum*.

"If we consider, on the basis of what we have thus far fully ascertained, the person of the Redeemer, we have, in the first instance, the genuineness of his human and divine nature. For his human nature is perfectly homogeneous with ours. Sprung from our race, consisting of body and soul, having the properties of a creature, capable of suffering, mortal: feeling, thinking, willing in the manner of men, but without sin. It is true that it does not possess the same originalness and independence as the divine, but it has in the latter the principle of its existence and subsistence. And this constitutes the truth of our Church's doctrine of the ἐνὑποζασια. If the case were otherwise, we would, in the place of a God-man, have a mere man, of whom we could only affirm that he is enlightened and animated by the divine. The objection, however, that in this way the humanity is deprived of an integrating element of its being, particularly of personality, falls to the ground of itself, according to the view which we take of the subject. For an absolute self-dependence or independence is not, at any rate, an attribute of human nature, but it is in all its members, and in every respect, determined in its condition by God, and is so far from being impaired or infringed upon, by this want of self-dependence that through this, precisely, it is what it is. Its peculiarity is dependent upon this, that it bears within itself a divine fundamental element of life. The same is true of the Redeemer, of whose life the Logos is the fundamental element. The only difference is this, that in him life is eternal, absolute, self-existent, and identical with that of the Father, (The Word of life), 1 John 1 and 2. (God, the Word, as the ancients correctly expressed it), eternal life. John 5:26: "life in himself," whereas in us it exists as life from God, limited as pertaining to creatures in a finite form, so that therefore, his being and ours are really of a kindred nature, ours being spirit of his spirit, life from the fullness of his life. But do we not thus fall into the error of the ancient Apollinarism, which denied that the Redeemer had any human personality? Not by any means. For that divine fundamental element of life within us, whose union with our animal nature is alone competent to produce human self-consciousness, and to give it reality, to fit us for the knowledge of God and for conscious communion with him, and to effect these in reality, is not itself, in fact, either the one or the other of these, but the basis upon which they are developed. This fundamental element of life does not, in fact, develop itself, but man's thought and will grow up, as it were, into it, and thus only acquire their distinct character and their full import. In a similar manner the divine Logos constitutes, in the Redeemer, the basis of his human consciousness, the possibility of a humanly thinking and willing me, without therefore being this itself, or subsisting as a second distinct consciousness alongside of it; for he has, in his incarnation, humbled, emptied himself, and laid aside his divine consciousness, in order to resume it again in the form of the human.

This humiliation however, which constitutes him a real man, does not, on the other hand, in any sense infringe upon the reality of his divinity. For, self-limitation is nothing else than self-determination, and when the divine Self determines itself to exist in a certain manner, or to operate within a limit fixed by itself, when it appoints for itself a definite mode or limit, it does not thereby cease to be the absolute. The creation of the world, the production of personal beings with a free self-determination, together with the possibility of the fall, and the permission of evil; nay, the entire government of the world, in its patience and long-suffering towards sinners, are all acts of self-limitation; for here God abstains from the manifestation of his absolute power, without therefore giving it up; just as when, on the other hand, he punishes the wicked, and withdraws his blessing from them, he does not cease to be Love. But this divine self-limitation and self-humiliation is preeminently displayed in the entire scheme of salvation revealed in the Gospel, of which the incarnation is the central point. That to which the whole history of man's salvation points appears here in its highest perfection. The Son gives up the fullness of his attributes, the relation in which he stands to the world as its Creator and Ruler, the being equal to God, but only so far as their active exercise is concerned; he does not give up his divine being or essence. In laying aside his divine glory, he does not lose his oneness of being or essence with the Father. As to his essence he remains God, whilst he divests himself of the form of God.

If from this we proceed to consider, in the second place, the mutual relation between the divine and human in Christ, it necessarily follows from the definitions given above, that we dare not regard the two as connected together externally, or in a manner merely ethical; for in this way the one being Christ would again become divided into a duality of persons; or we would have to come back to that mere indwelling of the divine, which we have already rejected, as in itself utterly incompatible with the idea of the God-man. But absorption of the human nature, or its transmutation into the divine, is just as much out of the question, as he would thus utterly cease to be essentially like unto us. The view which we are giving excludes, of itself, both these modes of re presentation. They are, in like manner, at variance with Scripture, and moreover, they rob the whole work of redemption of its significance and value. For if the divine and human natures in Christ are only externally connected, all that he did and suffered can be predicated only of his human nature, and ceases, as merely human, to have any redeeming value; but if the human has been absorbed by and into the divine nature, his human activity loses all its genuineness, and becomes a mere semblance or feint, as taught by the Docetists. In opposition to these erroneous conceptions (Nestorianism and Eutychianism), the distinctions and definitions given by our Church are impregnably true: "In

Christ, the two natures, the divine and the human, are united, in the oneness of his person, without confusion, and inseparably." But the most weighty consideration is the oneness, the unity; for, ever since the act of the Hypostatic Union (*unio hypostatica*), it is entirely improper to ascribe to him two separate natures, a twofold consciousness, a twofold will; it is, on the contrary, One undivided person of the God-man (*una indivisa persona*), in which the divine and human natures so pervade each other, as that neither can be regarded, or so much as thought of, as existing by itself, i.e. alongside or outside of the other. (*Unio arctissima, intima, realis*). And here the declarations of our Confession claim our unqualified assent: "To the integrity of the person of the incarnate Christ pertains not only the divine, but also the human nature" (FC 8.11). And again: "The Logos is not separate from the flesh, nor the flesh from the Logos." But every abstraction, which seeks to keep the two natures separate, is obviously entirely wrong, because no such separateness is found in the actual person. Even the analogy of body and soul, which it is usual to adduce, is utterly useless for illustrating this connection. It is too external. The well-known similitude of heated iron, which, at all events, is inapplicable to spiritual things, is equally useless. Only the relation of the human spirit to soul and body, or of the Holy Spirit to the regenerated, presents a suitable point of comparison.

II. The *Communicatio idiomatum*

Such being the state of the case as respects the person of the Redeemer, it follows that the whole of his active life cannot be regarded as a double series of acts transpiring alongside of each other, inter locking, like two cog-wheels; on the contrary, just as his person is a true, living unity, so also are his consciousness, his inward life, and his external activity to be considered as strictly integral, and belonging equally to both constituents of his being. For, as we have shown above, the divine Logos has not reserved to himself a separate existence, and hence also no separate mode of action, alongside of, or exterior to, the human, but has, on the contrary, condescended to enter, in this respect also, entirely the form of humanity. And with this we have, at the same time, the possibility of a naturally-human development on the basis of the already given Hypostatic Union (*unio hypostatica*), from which that oneness of life can be more accurately explained according to its particular manifestations.

For even as in every human being self-consciousness exists potentially from the beginning, but attains to actuality only in the way of successive development, thus also the Redeemer had not from the beginning a developed knowledge respecting his divine-human being. In childhood his knowledge and consciousness are those of a child. But, as the consciousness of his innermost nature gradually unfolds itself to his view, the consciousness of his divine Sonship, of his relation to the Father, and of his call to be the Redeemer of the world, discloses itself to him at the same time; in a manner similar to that in which, with the progressive development of the spiritual elements of our nature, the consciousness of the relation in which we stand to God, and of our earthly destination, is disclosed to us. It is a process, therefore, in which the personality of the God-man is realized; but this process does not first effect the communion between the divine and human within him; this, on the contrary, being given, it proceeds from that which already exists, and only carries it onward to a state of consciousness. This consciousness itself is not, therefore to be partially regarded either as human, or as divine, but as integral, i. e. as *divino human*.[41]

---

[41] With the Redeemer, as with us, this development is mediately effected through the influence of the Holy Spirit, which affected him through all the divinely-ordered relations of his early life, and particularly through the word of his Father : there is here, however, this essential difference that, whilst ours is at all times passing through sin and error, his not only remained free from all pollution, but unfolded itself with a clearness and continuousness, by virtue of which every moment of his life, being

What is true of his consciousness is therefore true also of his entire life and activity. This is, like the former, integral, *divino-human*. What he speaks, feels, and suffers in the performance of his mediatorial office on earth, his sympathy with the misery of the world, his participation in the poverty and weakness of our nature, the conflict with temptation, his grief and suffering—all these purely human acts are at the same time divine, because they proceed from the one person of the God-man.

> Wherefore (though made so much better than the angels) in all things it behooved him to be made like unto his brethren, that he might be a merciful and faithful high priest in things pertaining to God. (Heb. 2:17)

"Though he were a Son [better: although he was the Son], yet learned he obedience by the things which he suffered." Heb. 5:8. And therefore also the Scriptures describe his whole work of redemption at one time as the work of the Son of Man, at another as the work of the Son of God. They say: "the Lord of glory"(designating his divine nature) is crucified, 1 Cor. 2:8, but also "the Son of man suffered in the flesh" (Luke 9:22). 1 Pet. 4:1; on the one hand they ascribe his sufferings to his human nature, and on the other they derive its efficacy to atone for the sins of the whole world, from its being the suffering of the Son of God; Cf. 1 Pet. 1:19-20. Matt. 20:28 with 1 John 1:7. "The blood of Jesus Christ, the Son of God" (Acts 20:18). For this very reason we do not suffer ourselves to be at all disturbed by the oft-repeated objection, that thus the divine nature in Christ is degraded

---

animated by humble obedience and holy love to God, contained within itself a living impulse to farther progress, so that, with Schleiermacher, we may regard the unfolding of his personality, from earliest childhood to the maturity of manhood, as an unbroken course of transition from the purest innocence to a perfect fullness of spiritual strength, which is widely different from everything that we call virtue.

into that which is human. On the contrary we teach, as the Scriptures do, not only a co-knowledge, but an actual participation, a real sharing in the same feelings and sufferings on the part of the divinity of the Redeemer, in respect of the condition and sufferings of his humanity,[42] nay, we regard this as a necessary consequence of the incarnation, and refer the entire significance of all that he did and suffered, precisely to this, that it is *divino-human.*[43] We comprehend what has been said above, in this aphorism: *What the Redeemer does as man he does also as God.*

But this truth directly includes within itself this other, that what he does as God, he does also as man. For, as the human life of the Son is actively manifested in and with the divine, so is his divine actively manifested only in and with his human life. The light, the truth, the power of the Logos so entirely pervade and illumine the human spirit, that no separation is here possible. What he thinks in his divine nature, he thinks at the same time in his human nature, just as his divine word is, in the strictest sense, human. Those manifestations of power, those acts which we are wont to ascribe, preeminently, to that which is divine in him; not only the miracles which he wrought in the days of his flesh, but also those far greater ones which he continues to work; the diffusion of light in the world (John 8:12), the victory over spiritual and physical death, the restoration of life John 5:21, John 11:25-26), the government of the Church, the communication of spiritual gifts and graces (Eph. 4:8), the

---

[42] The main force of the above-cited passages, Heb. 5:8, 6:15, cf. 2 Cor. 5:19. with Heb. 1:3, rests entirely upon his suffering being that of the Son of God.

[43] It is usual here also to appeal to the relation between body and soul. It is common to say that, when the body suffers, the soul suffers with it, but in a different manner. It would, however, be better to urge this fact, that the soul can suffer (sympathize) with the body, without being violently affected by this fellow-suffering. It can preserve, in the midst of it, its peace in God, its serene, equable spiritual life:—and thus also the divinity suffers with humanity, without losing its own eternal serenity.

bestowing of the bread of life (John 6:51), the raising of the dead, and the final judgment (John 5:27)—all these pertain also to his humanity, because they proceed from the one person of the God-man. The same being that suffers and dies, enlightens and animates the world — the same being that works miracles, shares also the poverty and the limited condition of the flesh. So far as the Logos possesses and exercises the divine glory, to the same extent he possesses and exercises it also as Man.

During the whole of his mediatorial activity on earth, however, this possession was limited. It is only at the close of his earthly career, that it attains its full measure and completeness, the glory, which the divine Logos had laid aside, is restored to him as the God-man, and thus, communicated also to his humanity.

We regret that want of space, as it forbade our presenting what precedes the extracts above given, prevents our translating the sections which follow, and in which the author shows how consistent, how unswervingly faithful to Scripture, the Church has been throughout, in carrying out these views with reference to both our Lord's state of humiliation, and his state of exaltation.

We had designed in our own manner and language to discuss this entire subject extensively, but, finding that we could not possibly condense what we had to say within a sufficiently narrow space, we abandoned the attempt. And, although the extracts above translated are only fragments of an extensive treatise, they are sufficiently complete and satisfactory to show what our Church believes in respect of the great theme, so strenuously assailed in the article before us. To offer such a statement seemed imperatively necessary, as Dr. S. shows no favor either to the doctrine of the hypostatic union, or that of the *communicatio idiomatum*, as taught by our Church. What, without the hypostatic union, his belief respecting Christ's person and work can be, and what, according to his views, is to become of the whole doctrine of the atonement, is more than we are able to comprehend. We believe that, if the Scriptures teach anything clearly, definitely and positively, they do thus teach the doctrine of the hypostatic union of the Divine and human natures in Christ. And we further believe, that from this doctrine, in connection with the words of the institution, the view set forth in our Confessions respecting the Lord's Supper necessarily follows, and is, accordingly, distinctly taught in Scripture.

> As Christ is a divine-human person, he is, wherever he is, personally, entire, undivided, not merely as God, but also as man; and this is especially true respecting the manner of presence, in which, as the exalted Redeemer, he dwells and operates in his Church.

Luther says:

> Distance and space do not divide the nature in him, which certainly neither death nor all devils can tear asunder. Where you tell me that God is, there you must also admit the humanity to be, for they cannot be divided or separated.

To this position he firmly adhered, without wavering, and this is the more to his credit, as he had strong temptations, which cost him great inward conflicts, to give up his views, because he well knew, that he could thus most easily give the doctrine of the sacrifice of the mass its death-blow. But he was not to be induced to do evil, in order that good might come thereby. "I confess," Luther writes in 1524,

> That, if Carlstadt or anyone else had been able to prove to me, five years ago, that there was nothing more than bread and wine in the Sacrament, he would have rendered me a great service. I have, in this matter, endured severe conflicts, have striven, and

turned myself hither and thither, to find my way out,
because I saw clearly, that thus I would be enabled to
give the papacy the hardest knock, but I am held
captive, and cannot get out; the text is too strong, and
words do not suffice to strip it of its meaning.

He would not and could not yield to arguments of human
reason, because the power of God's Word in the Gospels and
in the first epistle to the Corinthians held him bound. And
when the Swiss protested that it was a contradiction to say,
that Christ is in heaven and at the same time in the Eucharist,
he did not for a moment suffer this seeming incongruity to
perplex him, but argued in reply that, "both must be true,
because the Scriptures teach both." Human reasoning, and
objections invented by the ingenuity and wisdom of man,
could not lead him astray, even when plied with passages of
Scripture, which seemed to be contradictory. "The
Scriptures," he declared "cannot contradict themselves; and
because, according to them, Christ's body is present in the
Lord's Supper, it must be possible." And here we take, with
him, our stand, leaving to others the foundations laid by
human reason, if they please them better, and afford them
safety and peace.

CHAPTER 12
CONCLUDING ARGUMENTS

THE author of the article before us now proceeds, in paragraph 4 to present what he calls, "The second tropical Interpretation (by Calvin.)" With this we have no concern, as we are defending the doctrine of the Lutheran Church; and although we find here sundry points that are open to criticism, we cannot spare room, and therefore pass on to what is announced to be 5: "The true, Historical and Pauline interpretation of the Words of the Institution." The arrogance with which this rationalistic interpretation is put forward as alone true and historical, and even saddled upon St. Paul, would be ludicrous, if it were not so presumptuous. The great Apostle of the Gentiles would probably not have been very grateful for the compliment here offered to him. But let all this pass. There is, in this exegetical effort, a good deal that is irrelevant, or again, mere arbitrary assumption. To the general position here taken, we have already replied on the preceding pages. We have seen, that the arguments advanced against the correctness of the interpretation given by the Lutheran Church in her Confessions against the strictly scriptural soundness of this interpretation, are feeble and untenable. We maintain that the Lutheran interpretation is the only consistently literal one; that the doctrine of the perfect and inseparable union of the two natures in Christ, which constitutes the true basis of the doctrine of the atonement, involves equally the doctrine which we have been compelled to defend; and such being the case, this "true, historical, and Pauline interpretation" is neither true, nor historical, nor Pauline. After all that has been said, it would be quite unnecessary to examine and criticize this exegetical attempt in detail. We shall notice only a few particulars, and then conclude with a brief statement of the Lutheran view of the Lord's Supper.

The Doctor begins with the Passover, and insists that "it is the Lord's passing over" is equivalent to "it signifies the angel of the Lord's passing over." We should really like to be informed how the slain and roasted lamb was to signify the angel. Exodus 12 says nothing of his kind. Refer ring to Exodus 12:26-27 he says: "No one imagines these words to mean: The lamb that was slain at the Passover, was the passing over of the Lord's angel. All admit that 'is' here is equivalent to signifies." There are several points here which our author overlooks. The paschal lamb was slain as a sacrificial victim, and as such, eaten. It is not the lamb itself which is called the Lord's Passover, but (as appears from Exod. 12:26-27). the sacrificial meal or feast—the act of partaking of the flesh of the victim in the manner appointed,—the entire service, or, if any prefer, the sacramental rite; and herein is a true and unmistakable analogy between the type and the anti-type. And moreover, at the very time when that lamb was eaten, the Lord was passing over, and sparing Israel, so that the appointed rite exhibited a present reality.

Our author urges the figurative nature of the words of the institution again. In addition to what has already been said, here we merely transcribe a few sentences from his own translation from Reinhard, in the first edition of Storr and Flatt's Theol., vol. 2 p. 330, simply reminding the reader, that in that treatise the Dr. calls these views of Reinhard "lucid and philosophical." Reinhard purports that:

The context affords us not the least ground for supposing them to be figurative, which would have to be the case before we should be authorized to depart from the natural meaning of the words. In addition to this, we should make decided tautology of Luke 22:19, by explaining figuratively the words "this is my body" for their meaning would then be the same as that expressed by the succeeding words, "do this in remembrance of me." But that these last words are not an explanation of the preceding, is evident from the circumstance that they are given as a command. The same remarks apply also to 1 Cor. 11:24-25.

Although Reinhard is not strictly Lutheran in his views, the reader may consult, with advantage, the pages which follow this quotation because we do not have space for more. Again, we have another consideration to urge in respect of the words of the institution, philologically regarded as to their grammatical force and arrangement. The opponents of our doctrine maintain that the word "is" does not here really denote being, but that it means the same as "signifies," and that therefore it is not here employed in its proper sense. Now in view and denial of this assertion, we insist upon the well-known principle or axiom, long since established in accordance with the laws of thought and of language, that the copula, "is", never, in any sentence, admits of a trope or figurative mode of speech: i.e. can never itself be the vehicle of a trope or figure. For in every complete sentence in which the predicate is distinctly expressed, the copula "is" is always merely an adjunct or accessory of the predicate, and never independently predicating. Hence the figurative signification can never be carried or conveyed by this word alone, but it must, if really intended, lie either in the subject or in the predicate, while the verb or copula is, in reality, in no way concerned or connected with the intended figure of speech. Now let this axiom, the correctness of which cannot be questioned, be applied to the words of the institution of the Holy Eucharist, and also to other passages which Zwingli, who has, in this, found a host of imitators, was wont to cite in favor of his view.

If the words of the institution really presented a figurative use of any word, this would have to be contained either in the predicate or in the subject. The predicate in the body and the blood of Christ, but of these words there cannot here be any unreal use, because, if this were the case, it would follow that an unreal body had been crucified, and unreal blood shed for us; and, if this were true, then would also the entire salvation of man be something figurative, something unreal. Nor is a figurative use of the word any more admissible in respect of the subject. This is, in the one case, the bread, in the other, the wine, respecting which no argument is necessary to prove that they are not to be taken figuratively or unreally. There cannot, therefore, in the words of the institution, be an unreal, unliteral, figurative use of a word, as it lies neither in the predicate, nor in the subject, nor in the copula, "is."

But Zwingli and his followers and imitators have cited other passages, in which, as they conceive, the verb "to be" is employed in the sense of "to signify." By applying the principle or axiom above cited to these passages, their correct interpretation is secured. For although there obviously is, in all these passages, a trope or figure of speech, this does not lie, is not contained, in the copula "to be," but either in the subject or the predicate. Thus, when it is said 1 Cor. 10:4 "that rock was Christ," the subject, "the rock," is to be taken unreally, figuratively; for here no material, earthy rock is intended, but that "spiritual rock," which followed the Israelites in the desert, and this rock the Lord Jesus did not signify, but he was that rock indeed and in truth. In the same manner are to be understood the passages: Matt. 13:38, and Rev. 1:20.

But in the words found in Matt. 11:14, a figurative predicate is undoubtedly employed. "And this is Elijah." This does not mean that John the Baptist was really, actually, Elijah, but that "Elijah, which was for to come." In like manner explain John 15:1, where we again find a figurative use of the predicate: "I am the true vine," or 15:5: "I am the vine." These words do not mean: "I signify a real, earthly vine, but I am in truth that spiritual vine, from which flows eternal life into all that believe." Similar passages in the gospels, containing similar declarations of the Savior, are to be explained in the same way. And thus also, in the words Gal. 4:25: "For this Hagar is Mount Sinai," the predicate is used in an unreal, tropical sense; for St. Paul intends here to say, that what occurred on Mount Sinai is also to be affirmed of Hagar and her son. For even as, on that mountain, the law was given, which pronounces the condemnation of the sinner and his expulsion from the presence of God, but comprises, at the same time, the promise and the future redemption, so the same thing happened to Hagar, for she also was expelled from the dwelling of her child's father, and received the promise respecting her son.

And thus it is obvious and certain, that the verb "to be" is nowhere to be explained as meaning "to signify;" and least of all is this interpretation admissible in the words of the institution of the Holy Eucharist. This is alone sufficient to show that the words of the institution must be taken in their appropriate, literal sense, the words themselves admitting of no other. But, in addition to other arguments already advanced, still other reasons remain to be mentioned, which confirm and establish the correctness of this interpretation. And here we maintain, further, that if the entire structure of Christian doctrine is not be a tottering edifice, perpetually threatening to fall, a mass of ruins, to the ground, we must strictly adhere to the principle or axiom, that those words of the Sacred Scriptures, in which, as in its own seat and strong hold, any article of faith is fully expressed and completely contained, arc not to be understood in any other than their literal sense. And here we translate from Chemnitz[44] the following very satisfactory and conclusive train of reasoning:

> We know, indeed, that in the Sacred Scriptures there are some difficult and obscure passages, in the interpretation of which we are free to depart from the words, provided only we derive from them a meaning or sense that harmonizes with other passages of Scripture. But the case is totally different in respect of those passages of the Sacred Scriptures, in which an article of faith is conveyed, revealed and established, as in its real and appropriate seat. For if, in the case of these passages, we deviate from the words, forsaking that sense which the words, in their simple, natural and ordinary signification, yield and express, and resting satisfied with some other sense which, in one way or another, harmonizes with other passages of Scripture, no article of faith can remain fixed or certain. But it is a point not open to controversy, that the words of the institution are the true and proper seat, in which the doctrine of the Lord's Supper is conveyed, revealed and established. And when St. Paul repeats to the Corinthians these same words, he gives them, as it were, as a canon and rule, according to which all questions and controversies respecting this doctrine are to be decided. And we very well know that, in the Sacred Scriptures many things are said figuratively, which must be taken in an unreal sense, differing from the ordinary meaning of the words, and must be thus interpreted and understood.
>
> Yet it was not the will of God that a distinction of this kind should be made according to any private interpretation, but, to the end that it might be justly and correctly done, he caused one and the same doctrine to be repeated in divers places of

---

[44] Loci Theologici, p. 169

Sacred Scripture, so that, in consequence of the necessary copiousness of truth to be believed, the Holy Spirit himself either confirmed and explained, by these same repetitions, the literal meaning, or showed that the words were not to be taken in their proper sense, but to be understood in a sense different from that which they literally express. But now our opponents cannot even deny, that the words of the institution of the Lord's Supper, when taken in their simple, appropriate, natural signification in which they are ordinarily employed in the sacred Word, yield the sense, that that which is present, distributed, and orally received by the communicant, in the Sacred Supper, which is celebrated on earth according to the institution, is not only bread and wine, but at the same time also the body and blood of Christ. And though the words of the institution are repeated in the Holy Scriptures at four different places, and the doctrine is also expressly repeated in several other passages, yet it is nowhere shown, by a direct and definite argument, that the simple, appropriate and ordinary sense of the words is to be departed from; but the meaning, which the literal interpretation of the words affords, is, on the other hand, fixed and confirmed in these repetitions.[45]

Again, see our author's article, p. 55. The entire argument against the Lutheran interpretation, here derived from the breaking of the bread, is impertinent and entirely gratuitous. That Christ's body should be broken, was determined from the foundation of the world; when the Holy Supper was instituted, it was on the eve of being broken, if it had not

---

[45] This argument, and the preceding based upon the impossibility of the copula "is" serving as the vehicle of a trope, are substantially derived from an admirable little work by Doct. Emil Francke, entitled: "Die Lehre vom heiligen AbendmahL' Leipzig, 1843.

been broken, the world would not have been saved; and, though the breaking of the bread signify, or symbolically represent the breaking of the Savior's body, this cannot prove that the Sacrament is not, what the Savior and St. Paul say it is, and as the Savior declares, that this Sacrament is his body and blood, that in it communicants receive his body and blood, we must look upon all such interpretations as that before us, as arbitrary misinterpretations, and hold with Luther that in the Eucharist:

> The real, substantial, or natural body and the real blood of Christ are present; and that the same body which once was broken for us, the same blood which once was shed for our sins, and which now are glorified; not in the same form or mode, but in the same essence and nature.

Again: p. 56., 2. This whole argument, designed to show that commemoration is the sole design of the Lord's Supper, is mere speculation, and not less absurd than if we were to argue that, because flame is designed to give light, therefore it cannot be intended to be hot, and to communicate heat. And as we have shown, that the literal interpretation given by the Lutheran Church is alone correct, just and consistent, we cannot see how any further *onus probandi* can rest upon us, as regards the reception of the Savior's body and blood by communicants. Our author here loses sight entirely of the fact, that the Sacrament is, according to the words of the institution, and the strong language of St. Paul, to be viewed under two aspects, objectively and subjectively. The objective character of the Eucharist depends, in no way, upon our viewing it correctly, or faithfully remembering the sacrifice for our sins; but the subjective benefit, the unspeakable blessing which we are to derive from partaking of the elements, depends upon our subjective position, as worthy or unworthy communicants; as duly discerning the Lord's body or not, as suitably remembering, or indifferently disregarding, what he suffered, how he died for our sins, all which is sufficiently obvious from St. Paul's language. 1 Cor. 11:29; although our critic, for the sake of supporting his argument, presumes to intimate, on p. 59, that communion and recollection are synonymous terms. How is it possible to place any reliance upon exegetical principles that admit of such interpretations of language? A similar instance of exegetical license we find on p. 58, in these words:

> The Lord Jesus, the same night in which he was betrayed, took bread, and when he had given thanks, he broke it and said, Take, eat, this is my body which is (or is to be) broken for you.

What are we to think of such interpolations? And again, on page 61., he cites a number of Scripture passages to show that his interpretation of "is," as meaning "signifies," is correct: and according to this principle of interpretation we must, of course, read: The Lord signifies my rock and my fortress, signifies my buckler, signifies the horn of my salvation, signifies my high tower. The Lord signifies my shepherd, etc. If these readings, substituted for the "is," which, in every instance cited, denotes a great and blessed reality, can afford our author any comfort and edification, even so let him read for his own special benefit.

There is but one point more, belonging to this "Pauline Interpretation," for which we can make room: it is the third, at the bottom of page 58. There is here a great glorifying over the words; "For, as often as you eat this bread, and drink this cup you show the Lord's death till he come." Our author evidently imagines that this passage, or rather his exposition of it, must put an end to all further discussion, by hermetically sealing the mouth of every confessional Lutheran. Among other things he says:

> This declaration of the apostle is of incalculable value. The greater portion of the language of Christ is or

may be figurative, and therefore admits of a diversity of interpretations, and it may remain questionable which is their true sense. But this language of Paul is literal, nothing figurative about it, and therefore in its import all agree. All admit that he designs to say, as often as you celebrate this Holy Supper, you commemorate, perpetuate the memory of, revive the recollection of the death of Jesus on the cross.

Now this is truly a most amazing affair. The impression made upon us by this paragraph is, that the Doctor's principles of interpretation are rather unsettled, or that he is unfortunate in applying them. For it so happens, that it is precisely in this aspect, which these words of the apostle exhibit, that the Eucharist is symbolical; it is here that the apostle's language is figurative. Does Dr. S. mean that, by eating bread and drinking wine, we literally show the Lord's death? If not, then he means nothing. In our humble opinion this could be literally done, only if we had him bodily under our hands, and could nail him bodily to the cross: or, to say the least, if we could exhibit to men his lacerated, bloody, lifeless body, substantially, just as it was taken from the cross. But we shall be told that καταγγελλω signifies to announce, to publish, as well as to show forth. Very well. We put it to the common sense of all men to decide, whether eating bread and drinking wine is the customary method, or (except when known to be specially appointed for this end) any intelligible method at all, of announcing or publishing to men that any one has died, and died a cruel and painful death. Of course we do not for a moment question the importance and significance of this act, the admirable adaptedness of the rite to show forth the Lord's death, and the manner of it, among those who are instructed in gospel-truth, but does it tell anything to those who are not thus instructed? It is precisely in this respect, and not as the communion of the body and blood of the Lord, that this rite is symbolical, and the language employed to describe it, figurative, requiring to be fully explained to those who are not already acquainted with the gospel history and scheme. Even Dr. S. enters into an explanatory paraphrase, in the last sentence above quoted, in which the announcing, publishing, and showing forth are overlooked, and the whole significance of the celebration is referred to the communicants themselves.

The remaining matter here presented, and coining under the same category, has already been sufficiently discussed on former pages. As respects the precious specimen of exegesis commencing near the bottom of page 62, we may safely let that stand to speak against itself; it needs no comment; but if this mode of amplifying and paraphrasing Scripture is to come extensively into vogue, and to be employed for the purpose of construing out of the Scriptures such doctrines as human reason or prejudice is disposed to quibble at, the sooner we burn our Bibles the better.

In the view which our author presents in conclusion, of what he actually finds in the Holy Supper, we notice in a very few words, only two points. Firstly: A spiritual presence of the Savior as to his human nature, is nonsense, and the additional word symbolic plainly denotes that the author really meant no presence at all, so that he can safely omit this article, if ever he publishes a second edition of his confession concerning the Eucharist.

Secondly: His "influential presence" is condemned by the objection which he himself, and that unjustly, makes on p. 50-56, to the Lutheran view. This influential presence amounts to nothing more than the influence of the ordinary means of grace, and has therefore again nothing particular to do with the Lord's Supper. This mere operative presence, borrowed from Reinhard and Storr, has the entire letter and spirit of the words of the institution, of John 6 and of 1 Cor. 11 against it. Whatever name, style or title may be given to the summary view of the Lord's Supper, here alleged to be the most scriptural, nothing can be more certain than this, that the Lutheran Church can have nothing to do with it.

That the Lutheran view of this Holy Supper involves a great and profound mystery, we not only admit, but we contend that without this there is no Sacrament. If the opponents of our scriptural view call upon us to explain this mystery, and the idle demand is often made, we promise to make the attempt as soon as they have succeeded in explaining the smallest mystery in the natural world around them, e. g. of the development and growth of a blade of grass. The revelations of God, in nature and in his Word, are full of mysteries which no finite intellect can explain or fathom. The scheme of redemption has vast and glorious mysteries in its wonderful doctrines, at which human reason is not to stumble, because it cannot gauge and explain them, but which the soul is simply to believe, that it may be saved. Among these glorious mysteries is the doctrine concerning the presence of our Lord's glorified humanity in the Eucharist, which we believe simply because the Scriptures teach it. That theologians should have employed the doctrines of the hypostatic union and the *communicatio idiomatum*, as clearly revealed in God's Word, to prove that the Church has correctly understood the Savior and his apostles, was merely discharging a duty laid upon them by the efforts of opponents, but with this the mystery is not intended to be explained.

We shall therefore, in conclusion, merely state, what the Sacrament of the Altar is to us, and, in so doing, we shall employ, not our own words, but the language of eminent and celebrated divines of our Church. We give, in the first instance, from Johann Gerhard's great work, Tom. 5., p. 55, the following clear and succinct statement.

> This presence is not an essential transmutation of the bread into the body, and of the wine into the blood of Christ, which they call transubstantiation, nor is it a local and .permanent junction (or union) separate from the sacramental use, of the body with the bread and of the blood with the wine (See Augsburg

Confession de Abus. I., Form. Cone. pp. 749, 750, 756), nor is it a personal union of the bread and the body of Christ, such as is the union of the divine and the human nature in Christ; nor is it a local shutting up of the body in the bread; nor is it impanation, nor an incorporation into the bread; nor is it consubstantiation, whereby the bread coalesces with the body of Christ, and the wine with the blood into one physical mass; nor is it a natural existence of the body and blood in the bread and wine, nor a concealment of the body, in a diminutive form, under the bread, nor any such carnal and physical thing ; but it is a sacramental presence and union, which is of such a nature, that with the bread, consecrated according to the institution of the Savior, the body of Christ is, as by a means divinely ordained, united and with the consecrated wine, as by a means divinely ordained, the blood of Christ is united, in both instances in a manner to us incomprehensible, so that together with that bread we receive and eat, by a sacramental manducation (eating) only, the body of Christ, and together with that wine we receive and drink, by a sacramental drinking only, the blood of Christ. In short, we hold that in the Sacred Supper there is, not absence, nor existence within, nor consubstantiation, nor transubstantiation, but the real presence of the body and blood of Christ.[46]

To this statement, by which every possible misconception is as carefully and effectually guarded against as language will admit, we subjoin the following brief exhibition from Quenstedt, 4, page 194. "A presence super-physical, illocal, not subject to any inclusion, extension or expansion."[47] It will

---

[47] "Praesentia hyperphysica, illocalis, omnisque inclusionis, extensionis, et expansionis expers."

be perceived, at once, that here no attempt is made to explain the great and sacred mystery of the Eucharist: all that is aimed at, is, to state distinctly and accurately what the doctrine of the Church is not, and what it really is. Having thus quoted two of our earlier Fathers, we shall now conclude with the following citation from the recent work of Sartorius, "*Lehre von Christi Person und Werk*":

> The Savior could indeed have been always and everywhere spiritually present with his disciples, in his divine nature; but this general, invisible, incomprehensible presence could not at all guarantee for them his peculiar, definitely circumscribed, human presence. Moreover, it was not only as God that he desired to be present with them, but he also desired constantly to communicate himself to them as the God-man or Mediator, to give himself to them as their own, and to receive them into communion with himself. This could not be affected through that divine omnipresence. And therefore he appointed or established, in the Sacred Supper, a special divine-human presence of himself in his Church, when he says, in the most explicit words, respecting the bread of the altar: "this is my body;" and respecting the wine: "this is my blood." By these same words he connects his invisible, incomprehensible, gracious presence, with the visible, comprehensible elements of the bread and the wine; so that, at the Sacrament, we are not to seek it in heaven or anywhere else, but precisely there where he has himself fixed it, i.e. in the elements of the Sacrament, in the bread and wine. Here then Christ is present for us; not, however, merely externally, but he gives himself to us to be our own, our highest good, and communicates himself unto us, inwardly, as our Savior, through the participation of the elements. Not as though a transmutation of the bread and wine into his body

and blood took place, as the Romish Church teaches; by no means; as in the incarnation of the Son of God, human nature was not transmuted into Deity, no more are bread and wine converted into the substance of Christ; but, as there, so here, there is only an intimate union, which is indeed supersensuous, but yet real and substantial, according to the promise of Christ.

And on this promise we intend, to abide, for it abides, and stands firm and sure forever.

Made in United States
Troutdale, OR
12/12/2024